# Fermented Foods vol. 1: Fermented Vegetables

## Written by Meghan Grande

Part 1 of **The Food Preservation Series** of Books

## **Disclaimer:**

The information contained in this book is for general information purposes only.

While we endeavor to keep the information up to date and correct, we make no representations or warranties of any kind, express or implied, about the completeness, accuracy, reliability, suitability or availability with respect to the book or the information, products, services, or related graphics contained in the book for any purpose. Any reliance you place on such information is therefore strictly at your own risk.

None of the information in this this book is meant to be construed as medical advice. Always consult with a medical profession prior to making any dietary changes in your life.

# Contents

Introduction ..................................................................... 6

Bacteria in the Gut .......................................................... 8

Restoring Good Bacteria to the Gut ............................. 13

Fermented Foods Are Alive .......................................... 17

Fermented Foods Are More Nutritious ........................ 20

Die-Off: Toxins in the Body ......................................... 22

The Many Health Benefits of Fermented Foods .......... 24

Buying Fermented Vegetables vs. Making Them Yourself .......................................................................... 27

Fermenting Preserves Vegetables ................................. 30

Safety First: How to Ensure Your Veggies Stay Safe .. 33

Fermenting in 5 Easy Steps ........................................... 37

How to Make Brine ....................................................... 39

What Type of Salt Works Best? .............................. 41

What Type of Water Should Be Used? .................... 42

Starter Culture: Give Your Fermenting Vegetables a Boost ............................................................................... 44

Fermentation Equipment: The Supplies You're Going to Need ............................................................................... 47

Fermenting Vessels ................................................. 48

Kraut Pounder (aka Cabbage Crusher) .................... 52

Weighting Systems .................................................. 53

Cutting Instruments ................................................ 55

How to Tell When Fermenting Is Complete ............... 56

Don't Forget to Burp Your Airtight Jars ................. 59

Fermenting Recipes ........................................... 61

Easy Sauerkraut ............................................. 62

Fermented Coleslaw ........................................ 64

Sweet & Sauerkraut ........................................ 65

Traditional Kimchi .......................................... 67

Daikon Radish Kimchi ..................................... 69

Curtido ........................................................ 71

Fermented Kale and Cabbage ............................. 73

Fermented Asparagus ....................................... 75

Fermented Brussels Sprouts .............................. 77

Fermented Garlic Radishes ................................ 79

Cultured Carrots ............................................ 81

Fermented Ginger Carrots ................................. 82

Dilly Carrots ................................................. 84

Dilly Beans ................................................... 86

Dilly Sugar Snap Peas ...................................... 88

Fermented Onions ........................................... 90

Lactofermented Yellow Summer Squash ................. 92

Zucchini Pickles ............................................. 94

Sweet Pickles ................................................ 96

Fermented Vegetable Medley .............................. 98

Layered Veggies ............................................ 100

Pickled Mexican-Style Vegetables............................ 102

Pickled Peppers ....................................................... 104

Habanero Hot Sauce................................................. 106

Cultured Green Tomatoes ......................................... 108

Cultured Grape Tomatoes ......................................... 110

Lacto-Salsa .............................................................. 112

Fermented Salsa Verde............................................. 114

Lacto-Ketchup.......................................................... 116

Lacto-BBQ Sauce..................................................... 118

Cultured Horseradish................................................ 120

Fermented Walnut Pesto ........................................... 122

Fermented Garlic Cloves........................................... 124

Miso-Fermented Garlic ............................................ 126

Fermented Garlic Scapes........................................... 128

Beet Kvass................................................................ 130

Frequently Asked Questions ....................................... 132

Works Cited ................................................................ 137

# Introduction

From the outside looking in, fermented foods can be a bit intimidating. Fermenting is a foreign concept to most people and it appears to go against the basic precepts of food safety. We're taught from a young age not to leave food out or it'll spoil, and leaving food out is exactly what you're told to do in order to ferment it.

While it's true the fermenting process requires you to leave food at room temperature in order to ferment it, fermenting doesn't cause food to go bad. Instead, it does the exact opposite and actually improves the nutritional value of the food by adding healthy probiotic bacteria that rebalance your gut and are thought to improve your overall health.

We've been raised in a sterile world and most people begin to worry when they hear the word bacteria. After all, we use antibacterial soaps, face washes, detergents and a number of other products to get rid of bacteria. Why would we want to grow them and eat them?

Not all bacteria are bad. In fact, your body requires large numbers of bacteria in order to function. If all the bacteria in your body died today, you wouldn't be too far behind them. You need bacteria and they need you. It's a symbiotic relationship that benefits both parties, as long as you take the right steps to help good bacteria thrive and to keep the numbers of bad bacteria in check. Fermenting vegetables and other foods and consuming large amounts of good bacteria as we eat these foods is one of the ways you can help good bacteria maintain control.

It may all seem foreign at first, but fermenting foods is just like any acquired skill. Once you've mastered the basics it really isn't all that difficult. Vegetables are particularly easy to ferment because they require little preparation and are fairly forgiving when mistakes are made.

That's why I chose vegetables for this first book in a planned series of books on fermented foods. Once you've learned the ins and outs of fermenting vegetables, it won't be difficult to move on to other fermented foods like fermented milk products, kefir and fermented fruits.

# Bacteria in the Gut

Hippocrates once said, "All disease begins in the gut." While this may not have been completely true, his statement was a lot closer to reality than most people gave him credit for at the time. In fact, it wasn't until recently that scientists started to get a grip on just how important the gut is when it comes to the health of the rest of the body. Research done in the last few decades appears to prove gut health is tied to the overall health of the body in a number of ways and scientists are finally starting to come to terms with how to best manage the gut in order to keep the rest of the body running like a well-oiled machine.

To put it simply, your digestive tract is one of the most important systems in your body. We tend to take it for granted, other than those times when it acts up and we have an upset stomach or indigestion. Most people know the gut is responsible for digesting food, but they don't know much more than that. The digestive system does much more than just process food. It contains trillions of bacteria that play a key role in the health of your immune system. When the gut is unhealthy, the rest of the body typically follows suit, and a number of health issues and autoimmune diseases may begin to present themselves.

The microorganisms in the gut play a number of key roles when it comes to the health of the entire body. Here are just some of the many ways having a healthy gut is believed to positively impact your health:

- **Disease prevention.**

- **Improved digestion.**
- **Improved immune system health.**
- **Protection from candida overgrowth and yeast infections.**
- **Protection from food poisoning and harmful pathogens that enter the gut.**
- **Regular bowel movements.**

The impact of having an unhealthy gut can be severe. Gastrointestinal distress, diarrhea and bloating are just the beginning. Digestive issues can wreak havoc across your entire body, with problems potentially cropping up anywhere. Allergies, autoimmune diseases, acne, mood changes and even cancer some of the many health disorders and diseases scientists believe can pop up in the body when the gut isn't in good shape. If you're having health issues you can't figure out, you may need look no further than your gut.

Here's a small sampling of the many, many health issues believed to be associated with having poor gut health:

- **Acne.**
- **Alopecia.**
- **Anemia.**
- **Asthma.**
- **Bloating.**
- **A number of cancers.**
- **Chronic constipation.**
- **Diabetes.**
- **Diarrhea.**
- **Fatigue.**

- **Immune system diseases.**
- **Increased susceptibility to infectious diseases.**
- **Infertility.**
- **Intestinal disorders.**
- **Irritable bowel syndrome.**
- **Malnutrition.**
- **Neurological disorders.**
- **Respiratory infections.**
- **Yeast (candida) overgrowth.**

In addition to promoting good health, a growing number of doctors believe the microbes in the gut are tied to obesity and a number of scientific studies have attempted to make this connection. It's been postulated that the type of microbes that exist in the gut may be the reason some people seemingly pack on pounds at a faster rate than others (1).

While there is still a lot about the gut that isn't known, there are some things scientists agree on. There are more microbes in your body than there are cells. According to researchers, the gut contains around 100 trillion microorganisms (2). To put that number in perspective, if you were to wait 1 trillion seconds, you'd be waiting for 31,688 years. One hundred trillion seconds would leave you waiting for nearly 3.2 million years. In terms of money, if you had $100 trillion dollars, you would have to spend $100 million dollars a day for the next 1 million days in order to spend the entire amount.

At any given time, there are both good and bad bacteria in the gut. There are more than 400 species of good bacteria in the gut and they vastly outnumber the bad bacteria when conditions are optimal (3). The good bacteria, known as **probiotic bacteria**, keep the bad bacteria in check. In a healthy gut, the vast numbers of probiotic bacteria leave little room for the harmful bacteria and keep their numbers to levels the body can easily manage.

Problems start to arise when an event takes place that causes the number of good bacteria to drop off. All of a sudden the gut becomes a very inhospitable place. The harmful microorganisms suddenly have free reign and surge up to take the place of the good bacteria that are dying off. Pathogens may be able to pass through the gut into the rest of the body and the entire body's immune response is weakened. More resources have to be dedicated to the gut, so less help is available everywhere else. The worse shape the gut is in, the more likely it becomes there will be problems elsewhere in the body.

Here are some of the known factors that can contribute to the die-off of good bacteria in the gut:

- **Poor diet.** Processed foods and foods filled with sugar feed the wrong type of bacteria and yeast in the gut. They strengthen the number of harmful microorganisms and provide them the fuel they need to grow.
- **Antibiotics and antibacterial medications.** While these medications may be absolutely necessary for medical reasons, they tend to indiscreetly kill bacteria in the body and can kill off large numbers of good bacteria in the gut. Over-prescription and overuse of antibiotics can contribute to poor gut health.

- **Antibiotics in the food we eat.** Commercially-farmed fish, fowl and livestock are all fed antibiotics, some of which are passed into their meats and their milk.
- **Environmental toxins.** Heavy metals are toxic to bacteria. This can allow candida and other microorganisms to proliferate the gut as the beneficial bacteria start to die.
- **Excessive diarrhea.** If you have a condition that causes frequent bouts of diarrhea or are taking medicine that causes it, be aware that prolonged bouts of diarrhea can literally flush the bacteria out of your gut.

Keep in mind this is just a sampling of the many problems that can cause microbial imbalances in the gut. If you suspect you're suffering health problems as a result of a bacterial imbalance, consult with a physician as to the best course of action immediately.

# Restoring Good Bacteria to the Gut

If you do have a deficiency of good bacteria in the gut, I've got good news for you. You may be able to make a handful of dietary changes that will promote the growth of good bacteria and rebalance your gut. It isn't going to be easy, but with the guidance of a nutritionist who's well-versed in probiotic foods, it can often be done.

The average American consumes more than 150 pounds of sugar per year. That's at least 30 five-pound bags of sugar for every single person in the United States. Of course, we don't sit down with a spoon and a bag of sugar and go to town, but you get the point. There's hidden sugar in much of the food we eat and it's just as bad as eating sugar from the bag. No matter how you look at it, that's a lot of sugar—and that sugar feeds the bad bacteria and yeasts that exist in the gut. Avoiding sugar cuts off one of the main food sources for bad bacteria and can help the body begin to restore balance.

Processed foods and foods that are fried and/or high in fat can also wreak havoc on gut health and may be responsible for killing off healthy bacteria in the gut. Foods that contain allergens and are difficult for the body to process like unfermented dairy products and foods containing gluten can also cause problems in the gut. Instead of consuming large amounts of foods known to cause problems, it will benefit the gut to make the switch to healthy, natural foods instead. Fruits, vegetables, beans, seeds and nuts are all believed to be good for the gut.

Probiotic foods take things a step further by actually introducing beneficial organisms to the gut. That's right...probiotic foods are teeming with the bacteria a healthy gut needs to thrive. While the idea of eating foods that are full of bacteria may seem strange at first, rest assured probiotic foods contain the bacteria your body needs in order to function at a high level.

Unless you're actively seeking out probiotic foods, there's a pretty good chance your diet is sorely lacking in probiotics. Most of the food consumed under the Western diet has been pasteurized or otherwise treated in a manner that eliminates all bacteria. While this is great for manufacturers who don't have to worry about harmful bacteria proliferating the foods they sell, it's problematic for the people consuming large amounts of these foods because they aren't getting the bacteria they need as part of their diet.

This complete lack of bacteria in the diet is a relatively new occurrence. Fermented foods were commonplace in the diet at one time. In fact, fermenting is one of the oldest known methods of preserving food and natural fermentation was taking place long before man discovered it and started controlling it. It's safe to say fermented foods and natural bacteria have been a part of our diet for *millions* of years. Our ancient ancestors, and even our not-so-ancient ones, didn't worry about the bacteria that were on their food. They ate what they found and much of what they ate was covered in beneficial microbes.

It wasn't until the last hundred or so years that we started sterilizing our food and killing off all of the bacteria prior to packaging it and putting it on store shelves. Our foods, our bodies and our lives have been cleansed of much of the bacteria we need. I can't help but wonder if that's one of the contributing factors to the glut of health problems that have become prevalent since processed foods became the norm.

Bacterial flora won't readily regenerate once they've been eliminated. They have to be added back to the gut through either probiotic supplements or probiotic foods. Thinking of your intestines as a breeding ground for bacteria wouldn't be too far off. If you take a certain type of bacteria completely out of the equation, there's no way to produce that type of bacteria without reintroducing it to the breeding ground.

Probiotic foods and supplements may help the gut in the following ways:

- **The good bacteria in the probiotics replace bacteria the body has lost.**
- **The good bacteria crowd out existing bad bacteria, reducing the amount of bad microorganisms the gut has room for.**
- **The good vs. bad bacteria balance is restored to healthy levels.**

You'll never get rid of all the bad microorganisms in the gut, nor would you want to. They have their place and contribute to good gut health as long as they're kept in check and aren't allowed to grow out of control.

I'm of the opinion it's best to add bacteria to the gut through the foods we eat. Don't get me wrong. I have no doubt that there are effective probiotic supplements out there. There are a vast number of people using probiotic supplements for a variety of reasons, but it's important to realize the supplement market is largely unregulated and claims made by manufacturers may not be in line with what the products are actually capable of doing. If you do decide to take supplements, be aware the data on long-term safety of said supplements is limited and there may be risk of side effects, especially in those with underlying health concerns.

While probiotics may be able to help ease the effects of certain health conditions, they shouldn't be assumed to be a cure for anything. Dietary decisions are best made under the supervision of a physician or a doctor, so consult with your primary care provider prior to making any changes.

# Fermented Foods Are Alive

If you've never fermented anything before, you're in for a special treat. Fermented foods are living and breathing foods teeming with life. They're nothing like the sterile, boring foods you're used to. Fermented foods bubble, froth and create gases as part of the fermentation process and people are often surprised by just how dynamically alive (and pungent) fermented foods can be.

Fermented vegetables go through a transformation process known as *lactofermentation*. Natural lactobacteria that exist on the vegetables begin to feed on the sugars and starch in the food and they convert it to lactic acid, gases and small amounts of a bunch of other compounds. Just to give you an idea of the variety of lactobacteria that are involved, here are some of the many species known to promote fermentation in plants:

- *Enterococcus faecalis*
- *Enterococcus faecium*
- *Lactobacillus acidophilus*
- *Lactobacillus bavaricus*
- *Lactobacillus brevis*
- *Lactobacillus casei*
- *Lactobacillus curvatus*
- *Lactobacillus delbrueckii*
- *Lactobacillus fermentatum*
- *Lactobacillus lactis*
- *Lactobacillus plantarum*
- *Lactobacillus salivarius*
- *Leuconostoc mesenteroides*

- *Pediococcus pentocacus*
- *Streptococcus bovis*
- *Streptococcus thermophilus*

The exact amount of beneficial bacteria found in a single serving isn't known—and more than likely varies from vegetable to vegetable and from ferment to ferment, due to a number of environmental factors—but according to an article on Dr. Mercola's website, fermented vegetables produced using a starter culture were tested and were found to have 10 trillion units of bacteria (4). If this holds true across all fermented vegetables, eating a single serving will provide a megadose of beneficial bacteria.

Lactobacteria create *lactic acid* as a byproduct, which is largely responsible for the pungent smell and strong taste characteristic to fermented foods. The lactic acid preserves the fermented food because harmful microorganisms have a tough time growing in an acidic environment. Lactobacteria don't have this problem and are able to thrive. The fermentation process also adds enzymes, vitamins and a number of probiotic microorganisms to the food. It's the only food preservation process in existence that actually makes food healthier as it preserves it.

At times, fermentation can get vigorous. You'll actually be able to see bubbles rising to the top of the fermenting vessel. If you're using a completely airtight container, you'll sometimes hear pent-up gases escaping from the container when you take the lid off. I've heard of containers that were left sealed for too long that popped their lids, shooting them into the air and making a huge mess in the process. I can't say for sure this isn't an urban legend, but I have met individuals who claim to have witnessed it first-hand.

It's important to realize fermented foods are alive. Like any living creature, fermented foods are a bit on the unpredictable side. I like to tell people I'm introducing to fermenting that it's more of an art form than it is a science. You're dealing with live cultures and a food that's teeming with bacteria. There's no way to predict exactly how it's going to act, but once you learn the medium, you should be able to paint a pretty good picture.

# Fermented Foods Are More Nutritious

We touched upon the fact that fermented vegetables have increased nutritional value in the last chapter, but this is something that deserves a more in-depth discussion. Fermenting vegetables improves their health value in a number of ways. The fermentation process adds nutrients to the vegetables and it makes the nutrients that are already there more accessible.

Fermentation increases the amount of B-vitamins, folic acid, choline and glutathione in vegetables (5). B-vitamins are critical for energy, brain function and heart health. Folic acid benefits the brain, the colon and a number of other systems in the body. It's also been shown to help prevent neural tube defects in pregnant women (6). Choline helps the body regenerate cells and is a key component of a neurotransmitter the body uses to run the heart and keep the intestines in working order (7). Glutathione is an antioxidant used by the body to battle everything from cancer to heart disease. According to an article by Dr. Mark Hyman on the Huffington Post website: "It's the most important molecule you need to stay healthy and prevent disease" (8).

In addition to adding nutrients to food, fermentation partially digests the food and makes the nutrients that available in the food easier for the body to access. The digestive system can struggle to break down the fiber and cellulose material found in vegetables and may leave at least some of the nutrients behind as they pass through the digestive tract. Fermentation begins the digestion of these materials before they enter the mouth and way before they reach the digestive system. This jump-starts digestion, making it easier for the body to pull nutrients out of fermented foods.

# Die-Off: Toxins in the Body

When probiotics are first added to the diet, an event known as a *die-off* may occur. As probiotic bacteria move in and take control, they crowd out the harmful pathogens that were in control. This can cause large amounts of these harmful microorganisms to die-off at once, creating a crisis situation inside the body.

Bad bacteria release *endotoxins* as they die (9). The amount of toxins released by the death of a single bacterium is small and the body is able to quickly clear it out. As more and more bacteria begin to die, the detoxification systems in the body can get overwhelmed and the endotoxins can start to build up.

The body will eventually clear them out, but you may suffer symptoms from the die-off, including the following:

- **Aches and pains.**
- **Brain fog.**
- **Constipation.**
- **Diarrhea.**
- **Excess mucus.**
- **Fatigue.**
- **Fever.**
- **Gastrointestinal distress.**
- **Headache.**
- **Skin rashes.**

People who have gone through a die-off often compare it to having the flu or a cold. They say they feel run down and sluggish, as if the body is fighting off a nasty bug—and in a way, it is. According to most sources, this die-off usually lasts from a couple days up to a week before the symptoms start to subside. The symptoms can range from moderate to severe.

It's best to start off slow when adding probiotic foods to your diet. You don't know exactly how your body is going to react to the new food and you don't know what the bacteria population is like in your gut. An educated guess can be made based on your diet, whether or not you've been taking antibiotics or other medications and other risk factors, but the reality is you really don't know what things are like on the inside.

Don't dive into the deep end headfirst. Instead, it's best to dip your toes in the water. Because probiotic foods can have trillions of bacterial cultures in a single serving, it's best to start off with something much smaller than an entire portion. Sample a teaspoon of fermented vegetables and wait to see if there are any ill effects. If there are, eat an even smaller amount the next time. Once you find a level at which there are no ill effects, you can gradually start increasing the amount you eat every time until you reach a full serving. It's best to ease into such a drastic change in the gut.

Never assume changes in your overall health are due to a die-off. It's important to discuss any changes you notice with your doctor right away.

# The Many Health Benefits of Fermented Foods

There have been a vast number of health benefits attributed to fermented foods (and probiotics in general). This isn't just quack science. There are a number of new scientific studies that appear to back many of the claimed health benefits of fermented foods.

A review study published in 2005 in the Journal of Applied Microbiology indicates consumption of probiotics is associated with the following health benefits:

- **Control of inflammatory bowel diseases.**
- **Control of irritable bowel syndrome.**
- **Diarrhea therapy and prevention.**
- **Elimination of pathogens from the body.**
- **Enhanced immune system.**
- **Improved intestinal tract health.**
- **Improvements in the bioavailability of nutrients.**
- **Lower serum cholesterol.**
- **Reduced risk of certain cancers.**
- **Reduced symptoms of lactose intolerance.**
- **Reductions in allergy symptoms.**

The scientists who performed the study reviewed a number of other scientific studies and found there are a vast number of proven uses for probiotics that are well-documented in the scientific community (10).

Additionally, the website GreenMedInfo.com has amassed a collection of 245 scientific studies that look at various health benefits associated with probiotics. Links to the abstracts of the studies are available at the following web address:

http://www.greenmedinfo.com/substance/probiotics

Here's a small sampling of what the studies amassed by GreenMedInfo.com reveal:

- **A meta-analysis of more than 60 studies reveals probiotics are safe and are beneficial for treating infectious diarrhea (11).**
- **Lactic acid bacteria, in combination with other probiotics may play a role in reduction of eczema (12).**
- **Certain probiotics, when taken orally, were shown to be helpful in bacterial vaginitis treatment and relapse prevention (13).**
- **A dietary supplement containing probiotic bacteria, along with vitamins and minerals, was shown to reduce the duration, severity and frequency of contraction of the common cold (14).**
- **Fermented foods containing lactobacillus acidophilus may help alleviate allergic rhinitis, commonly known as hay fever (15). A separate study found lactobacillus casei also dampened the immune response associated with allergic rhinitis (16).**

There are many more studies available for you to take a look at if you're interested. Keep in mind scientists are just now starting to research the many health benefits of fermented foods and it's highly likely many more will come to light in the near future.

# Buying Fermented Vegetables vs. Making Them Yourself

I'm not going to beat around the bush here. You're almost always better off making fermented vegetables at home than you are buying them in stores. Of course I'm a little biased since this is a book about making fermented vegetables at home, but there are some pretty good reasons you should learn how to make them yourself.

For one, you have ultimate control over what goes into your ferments when you make them at home. You get to choose the vegetables you use and the herbs and spices you add and can ensure they're organic and are in prime condition. There's something to be said about being able to hand-pick your vegetables one at a time. I'm not sure what the quality control is like at the select few manufacturers who do make true fermented vegetables, but I'd be surprised if it's anywhere near as stringent as I am when picking vegetables for a ferment. You also get ultimate control over the rest of the ingredients used and can use as much salt, spices and other ingredients as you'd like.

Another key benefit is not having to worry about unnecessary ingredients added to the vegetables to improve shelf life or to make them look more presentable. There are manufacturers like BAO Food and Drink who use all organic ingredients, but you've got to keep a close eye on exactly what it is you're purchasing. If you read a label and find something other than vegetables, salt, water and spices, it's time to start questioning why that ingredient is in there.

Speaking of watching what you're purchasing, don't assume that just because the traditional version of a food is fermented and contains probiotic cultures, the store version will be same. There are a number of bastardized versions of normally-fermented foods that have been pasteurized or otherwise treated in a manner that kills off all of the beneficial bacteria.

Sauerkraut is a great example of this because much of the sauerkraut sold in grocery stores looks and tastes like sauerkraut, but is sorely lacking the probiotics you should be getting when you eat this tangy cabbage dish. Instead, you all-too-often end up with sauerkraut that amounts to nothing more than sour cabbage and vinegar. While it might taste similar, it's a far-cry from the probiotic goodness that is true fermented sauerkraut.

If you are going to buy fermented vegetables from the store, it's important to make sure you're actually getting fermented vegetables. Check the labels and make sure the label specifically says there are probiotic cultures contained inside. Manufacturers know this is a big selling point and will usually make sure it's prominently listed on the label. Be forewarned it can be a little tough to find true fermented vegetables on grocery store shelves unless you're lucky enough to live in a town with a natural foods store or a health food store nearby. Probiotic vegetables should be located in the refrigerated foods section, as leaving them on the shelves will allow them to continue to ferment at a fast pace. You might also be able to find them at a local farmer's market or at a fruit stand.

You might be shocked at the cost associated with buying prepared fermented vegetables, as they tend to be a bit on the expensive side. It's a little surprising, considering there are only a handful of ingredients that are all readily available, but a lot of work goes into making larger batches of fermented foods. It's difficult to control the fermenting process in smaller batches and this difficulty is amplified when the batches are increased to larger amounts.

Aside from the upfront costs of buying the fermenting vessels you need to get started, you'll save a lot of money by making your fermented vegetables at home as opposed to purchasing them premade. I've found that if I wait until I find a good sale on vegetables, I end up paying half or even a quarter of what it would cost to buy already-fermented vegetables. Making your own fermented foods is the better choice for budget-minded individuals with a limited amount of funds.

Another good reason to learn how to ferment vegetables is you open yourself up to a lot more variety. Even the best stores and markets only have a limited amount of refrigerator space available to dedicate to fermented vegetables and you're usually restricted to a few varieties of sauerkraut, kimchi and a handful of other vegetables. You can find more variety online, but if you're like me and are one of those people who prefer to buy food from a brick and mortar store, you're out of luck.

# Fermenting Preserves Vegetables

Most raw vegetables are prone to rapid deterioration once they're harvested. Many vegetables start to deteriorate within a few days of harvest and will deteriorate to the point they can't be eaten within a week or two.

Homegrown produce will last a little longer when it's harvested fresh from the vine, but home gardeners are often left with an abundance of produce they're forced to give away before it deteriorates too much to eat. Fermenting is a great way to preserve a large harvest in order to ensure you can enjoy the fruits of your labor for much of the year. There's no good reason to spend long hours in the garden only to have to start buying produce from the store within a short time after the harvest.

Fermentation slows the decomposition process of vegetables to a crawl by creating an environment in which the bacteria and microbes responsible for causing food to rot and go bad aren't able to easily grow. Raw foods that are left wide open to attack from harmful microorganism are enveloped in multiple layers of protection once they've been fermented.

Fermented vegetables are protected in several ways. Bad bacteria require an *aerobic environment*, which is an environment with plenty of oxygen available. The *anaerobic environment* in which fermentation takes place is largely devoid of the oxygen harmful microorganisms need to thrive. Probiotic microorganisms don't have the same oxygen requirements as their nefarious cousins and can get by with much less oxygen.

Salt is used in the fermenting process to further discourage the growth of harmful bacteria. Salt has been in use as a preservation agent since long before we had refrigerators and freezers to keep our food nice and cold so it won't go bad. Fermenting recipes typically call for a small amount of salt to be added to the recipe in order to prevent harmful microorganisms from growing until the lactobacteria are able to take over and go to work.

The lactobacteria create lactic acid, which creates an even more hostile environment for harmful bacteria. Lactic acid is a natural preservative that prevents the growth of the bacteria that cause food to spoil. It increases the acidity of the brine and helps preserve the taste, texture and color of the vegetables as they ferment.

So, just how long will fermented vegetables last? Vegetables that are fermented and then moved to cold storage can last months after the time they would have gone bad if left sitting on the counter. Moving your fermented vegetables to cold storage once they've undergone the initial fermentation period slows fermentation to a snail's pace. The food will still continue to ferment slowly, but it will be at a pace so slow it's almost unnoticeable.

You may be tempted to freeze fermented vegetables, but freezing them is out of the question. While lactobacteria can survive the cool temperatures of the fridge, they'll die off when subjected to the harsh cold of the freezer.

While fermented vegetables will eventually get too soft to be palatable, it's highly unlikely they'll spoil. I'm not going to go as far as to say spoilage never happens, because it most definitely does, but the odds are stacked against any bad bacteria attempting to gain a foothold. In my experience, when a food does turn, it's accompanied with an unmistakably foul odor and there are a number of signs the food has gone bad. Watch out for uncharacteristic changes and discard the entire batch of fermented vegetables if you notice something irregular.

# Safety First: How to Ensure Your Veggies Stay Safe

Properly fermented vegetables have a great track record in regard to safety, but it's important to realize things can and will go wrong if basic safety protocols aren't followed. Improper handling of fermented vegetables may allow pathogens to grow instead of the beneficial microflora you desire.

Safety begins well before you put your vegetables into the jar and begin fermentation. It's important to start off with sterile equipment and clean hands. Washing the jars, lids, knives and any other utensils you plan on using in a hot dishwasher or boiling them in a pot on the stove will help ensure you aren't adding harmful bacteria to your ferment before it gets underway. Similarly, it's important to wash your hands thoroughly. Be careful using antibacterial soaps on your jars, lids and utensils. Residues from these soaps may slow the growth of good bacteria as well as bad.

I prefer boiling all of the tools I plan on using for fermentation because it ensures they get hot enough to kill bad bacteria. I have a canner I use for canning fruits and jams, so I add water to the canner and place my jars in there. If you decide to go this route, boil the fermenting jars and lids for at least 10 minutes before pulling them from the water. It's best to boil them right before you plan on using them and to leave them in the hot water until you need them. That way, contact with open air and the risk of reinfection is kept to a minimum.

You might be tempted to attempt to give your vegetables a good cleaning before placing them in the fermenting vessel, but this isn't a good idea. The lactobacteria responsible for jump-starting the fermenting process grow in large amounts on the outside of most vegetables and a thorough cleansing will wash much of the bacteria away. It's much better to use organic vegetables for fermenting than conventionally-farmed vegetables because you don't have to worry about scrubbing away pesticide residue. A rubdown under running water is all most organic vegetables need as far as cleaning goes.

After you add the vegetables to the fermenting vessel, the brine you add to the fermenting vessel will inhibit the growth of harmful bacteria until the lactobacteria are able to take over. We'll cover brine in-depth in a future chapter, but for now just know brine is important because it creates an environment conducive to the growth of good bacteria and is prohibitive to the growth of harmful microorganisms. Not adding enough salt to your brine can allow pathogens to develop, but you also have to be careful not to overdo it. Too much salt will stop lactobacteria from growing as well.

Most fermented vegetable recipes call for enough brine to be added to where the vegetables are submerged beneath the brine. A weight is usually added to the container to ensure the vegetables stay submerged. This is to ensure fermentation takes place in an anaerobic environment. Vegetables that are allowed to float to the top of the container and are exposed to open air are much more likely to go bad.

Once the vegetables are submerged, the container must be sealed to prevent air from getting in. Airlock containers work great for fermenting because they have a one-way seal that keeps air out while releasing gas as it builds up in the container.

Temperature is the next consideration that must be made. The ideal temperature range to ferment most vegetables at is between 68° F and 75° F. Fermentation will be too slow below 68° F and pathogens may start to develop in the food. At temperatures above 80° F, fermentation will speed up too fast and food degradation will accelerate. Anything above 85° F can potentially kill the beneficial microbes you're trying to develop. This is dangerous because once the probiotic flora dies off; the food will be wide open to contamination from harmful microorganisms.

At times, you can seemingly do everything right and a ferment just doesn't seem to want to cooperate. As with any living, breathing thing, the microorganisms that exist in fermented foods aren't always predictable. While it doesn't happen very often, fermented foods can go bad. Here are some of the signs to look for that may indicate your vegetables have gone bad instead of fermenting:

- **The texture of the food is mushy or excessively slimy.**
- **Mold is growing inside the container.**
- **There is a putrid smell emanating from the container.**
- **The vegetables start to turn brown or develop dark spots.**

Your last line of defense when it comes to spoiled food is your sense of taste and the way the food feels in your mouth. If you go to eat something and it doesn't taste right or the mouthfeel of the food is off, spit it out and discard the rest of the vegetables and the brine in the container. Disinfect the container before using it again. The stakes are high when it comes to food poisoning and you're much better off starting over than you are eating something that could potentially make you sick.

Some sources indicate it's OK to remove a moldy layer of food from the top of a fermenting vessel and eat the layers of food below it that don't appear to be contaminated. You can probably get away with this because much of the mold that grows in fermented vegetables is harmless, but I don't do it personally because mold sends out invisible tendrils as it grows. The layers beneath the mold may be contaminated and the mold simply hasn't yet begun to show.

# Fermenting in 5 Easy Steps

*Lactofermentation.*

The first time I heard this word I was filled with trepidation. From the outside looking in, fermenting is a world clouded with intrigue. Creating foods that are teeming with bacteria is such a foreign concept in this day and age of pasteurization and sterilization that people assume it has to be excessively difficult.

I'm about to shatter that illusion.

It almost takes longer to spell the word lactofermentation than it does to prepare lactofermented vegetables. The 5-step process I'm about to reveal to you works for most vegetables and is easy enough almost anyone can do it. As long as you keep the basic safety rules in mind while following this process, you'll come out the other end with fermented vegetables that are filled with probiotic bacteria.

Here's the 5-step lactofermentation process:

1. **Sterilize the fermenting vessel.**
2. **Prepare the vegetables you want to ferment and place them into the vessel, along with any other ingredients you'd like to include.**
3. **Add brine to the vessel.**
4. **Seal the fermenting vessel.**
5. **Wait for fermentation to take place.**

That's it. While there are a handful of things you're going to want to keep in mind during the process, this 5-step process pretty much sums up fermentation. I could end the book right here and you could probably figure out how to ferment vegetables after a bit of trial and error experimentation.

Of course, the basic outline of the process leaves out a lot of the minutiae you're going to want to know in order to maximize your efforts. Like any acquired skill, fermentation takes a few minutes to learn and a lifetime to master.

# How to Make Brine

*Brine* is a critical ingredient for most fermented vegetable recipes. The salt in the brine, when used in the proper amount, inhibits the growth of bad bacteria, while allowing the lactobacteria the freedom to do their thing. Without salt, fermentation would have to be done in an extremely sterile environment to ensure safety. With it, you can relax a little, as brine creates an environment that's more forgiving because bad bacteria have a difficult time growing in salt water.

Salt also hardens the pectins in the vegetables and leaves them crunchier and packed with flavor (17).

Brine is usually measure by the percentage of salt found in the brine. 2% brine will contain 2% salt by volume. Most recipes call for brine that is between 2% and 5% salinity. Here's a chart you can use to ensure you're mixing your brine to the right salinity percentage:

| Percent Brine | Tablespoons Salt |
| --- | --- |
| 2% brine | 1 tablespoon |
| 3% brine | 1.5 tablespoons |
| 4% brine | 2 tablespoons |
| 5% brine | 2.5 tablespoons |

This chart assumes you're using a quart of water. If you're using more than that, you'll have to adjust your recipe accordingly.

For those who are sticklers about being exact, you can weigh both your water and your salt and then multiply the weight of the water by the percentage of salt you need to get the exact weight of the salt required. If you have 32 ounces of water and want 3% brine, you'd multiply 32 times 0.03 and end up with 0.96 ounces. This level of accuracy isn't necessary when dealing with quarts or even gallons, but some people prefer to be exact. It doesn't become critical until you're working with larger amounts of liquid, which you're unlikely to need to do when fermenting.

If you're concerned about using salt because you're sensitive to it or are on a salt-restricted diet, celery juice can be used in its place in most recipes.

## What Type of Salt Works Best?

There are only a small handful of types of salt you should use for fermenting vegetables. Here are the recommended salt types:

- **Unrefined sea salt.** This is the best kind of salt for fermenting because it contains natural nutrients. Himalayan sea salt is widely considered one of the best sea salts around and is the type of salt called for in the recipes in this book. It can be used interchangeably with the other types of salt.
- **Pickling or canning salt.**
- **Kosher salt.**

Steer clear of refined salts containing iodine, as it can mess with the fermentation process. Similarly, I'd steer clear of salt with any other additives. Processed salt often has an anti-caking agent added, which should also be avoided. You want your salt to be as pure as possible.

## What Type of Water Should Be Used?

Whenever possible, one should use as much of the natural juices of the vegetable being fermented as possible for the water source for the brine. Vegetables that have a lot of water like cabbage can often be chopped up and salted and they'll produce all the water you need within a few hours' time.

If you do have to add water, it's important you follow these two simple guidelines when choosing a water source:

- **The water should be free of toxins.** Chlorine and fluoride are to be avoided, so this eliminates most of the tap water in the Western world. If your water has chlorine, but not fluoride, you can let it sit for a day or two and the chlorine will dissipate. Stir it a couple times a day for best results. You can also boil the water for 20 minutes to get rid of any chlorine.
- **The water needs to be free of pathogens.** Just like you need to make sure your utensils and hands are free of pathogens, it's equally important to make sure your water is clean and free of pathogens.

Vegetable ferments can often survive in tap water that's been pulled straight from the tap, but your mileage may vary. If you're having trouble getting your vegetables to properly ferment, you may want to try switching your water source to one that's cleaner and/or contains less chemicals.

Mineral content isn't as important with fermented vegetables as it is with kombucha and kefir, but I've found my vegetables seem to ferment better in water that has at least some mineral content. As long as the salt you use is unrefined, it'll likely add minerals to the water as well.

# Starter Culture: Give Your Fermenting Vegetables a Boost

Most vegetables have all the lactobacteria you need for fermentation already crawling around on their skin or outer leaves. A number of home fermenters choose to ferment using only these bacteria in a process known as *wild fermentation*. With wild fermentation, vegetables are submerged in brine and fermented without any additional cultures being added.

Other fermenters choose to give their vegetables a gentle nudge in the right direction by adding what's known as a *starter culture* to the fermenting vessel at the beginning of the process. Starter culture comes in many forms and is something that contains the bacterial cultures you want to develop in the container. Using it speeds up fermentation and encourages the growth of the bacteria of the type that were added as starter culture. On the negative side, there are those who say you don't get as varied of a colony of bacteria when you add starter culture.

The following starter cultures have all seen use in vegetable ferments:

- **Brine from a previous ferment.** If you have a jar of fermented vegetables lying around, you can take some of the brine from the jar and add it to your new ferment to get it started. This usually, but not always, results in a ferment that tastes similar to the previous one.

- **Vegetable culture packets.** A handful of manufacturers sell packets of freeze-dried bacterial cultures. These packets typically create ferments that taste the same pretty much every time. This is great if you like the way they taste; not so great if you don't. A small amount of dairy may be used as a carrier for the bacteria, so make sure you read the label closely if you're sensitive to dairy.
- **Kefir grains.** Milk kefir and water kefir grains can be used to ferment vegetables, but they're a one-time use grain. People typically consume the grains at the same time they're eating the vegetables. Kefir grains are rather expensive, so you probably don't want to buy them just for this purpose. If you've already got kefir grains and are looking for a good way to use up extra grains you have on hand, it's worth a shot.
- **Whey.** Strain buttermilk or cultured yogurt through cheesecloth and the liquid you're left with is whey. This whey is filled with probiotic cultures and can be used as starter culture. It is a dairy product, so if you're sensitive to dairy, go with one of the other options.

You can generally sub one of the other types of starter culture into recipes that call for a specific starter culture. For starter cultures, a single packet is usually all that's needed for all but the biggest ferments. A few tablespoons to half a cup of whey are fairly standard. If you're using kefir grains, start with a tablespoon or two of grains. A cup of brine from a previous ferment usually works pretty well.

I'd recommend using starter culture to anyone who's new to fermenting. It speeds up the fermentation process and adds an additional layer of protection by boosting the amount of probiotic cultures in the ferment from the get-go. If you decide you want to experiment with wild fermentation, wait until you've got a bit of experience under your belt.

# Fermentation Equipment: The Supplies You're Going to Need

Here's a list of the basic supplies you're going to want to have on hand before getting started:

- **A fermenting vessel.**
- **A kraut pounder or similar blunt object.**
- **A large bowl.**
- **Cutting board.**
- **Cutting instruments (knives, food mandolins, etc.).**
- **A weighting system for your vessel.**

Let's take a closer look at some of the equipment you may not be familiar with.

# Fermenting Vessels

The biggest and most expensive item (or set of items) you're going to need is the fermenting vessel (or vessels, if you're using small jars). The *fermenting vessel* is the container the vegetables are stored in while fermentation takes place.

Picking the right type of vessel can be confusing, since there's no shortage of vessel types to choose from. The vast number of vessels on the market can lead to a lot of confusion amongst consumers who aren't sure what the differences are between the numerous types of containers.

There are several basic features you're going to want to look for in a vessel:

- **Round vessels work better for fermenting than rectangular vessels.**
- **Glass or ceramic works better than wood, metal or plastic.** Wood containers have nooks and crannies that are difficult to clean and can harbor bad bacteria. Plastic can leach chemicals into the brine and can contaminate the vegetables. Metal containers are off-limits because the metal can react with the lactic acid and the salt in the brine.
- **The vessel should be able to be sealed to prevent oxygen from entering the vessel.** Allowing air to get inside the container is never a good thing. A sealable lid will also prevent insects and animals from getting into the container.

When you start shopping around for fermenting vessels, you're going to find a large number of vessels that meet these criteria. They'll run the gamut from simple, inexpensive jars to intricate containers that cost a small fortune. While some of the expensive options are nice to have, there's to spend a small fortune unless you really want to. Fermenting has been done in simple containers for thousands of years. In fact, much of the fermenting done in the past was done in large, open barrels. Knowing what we now know about food safety, fermenting in open containers isn't a great idea, but it just goes to show the container doesn't have to be anything fancy.

Prior to the invention of airlock containers, most people who fermented vegetables did so in glass canning jars or similar glass containers. In fact, a lot of people still use glass jars for fermenting vegetables because they're inexpensive and most people already have at least a few of these jars put up somewhere in the house. There has been a handful of detractor of late claiming Mason jar ferments aren't safe because the jars aren't completely sealed and some oxygen may get in. At least three of the leading experts in the world of fermentation have gone on record stating that fermenting in mason jars is fine as long as you take precautions to ensure the vegetables stay below the surface of the brine (18).

This makes sense to me. As long as the vegetables are below the brine, they're in an anaerobic environment. I can't say it's never happened, but I will say I've never heard of anyone getting sick from fermenting using Mason jars— and there are a lot of people who still use them. If you do decide to go this route, use common sense. If a fermented food looks, smells or tastes off, don't eat it.

If all this talk of food safety has you worried about using Mason jars for fermenting, don't worry. There are plenty of other choices. *Airlock containers* are a popular choice, since they provide an airtight seal and have a built-in one-way gas release valve that prevents pressure from building up in the vessel. Airlocks use a water barrier to prevent air from making its way into the vessel. Gases that build up inside the vessel create pressure that pushes through the water barrier once it reaches a certain point. This release of pressure only works in one direction because outside air isn't able to force its way in. Airlock vessels are beneficial in that you don't have to open the vessel periodically to off-gas it, exposing the contents inside. You also don't have to worry about fermenting liquid spraying everywhere when you open the container.

There are airlock containers available that screw onto Mason jars or you can go all-out and buy the expensive versions from companies like Pickl-It or Cultures for Health. I like the commercial airlock jars because the lids are made from food-grade plastic and I don't have to worry about them coming in contact with the food.

Ceramic fermenting crocks are available for those looking to ferment larger amounts of food. They tend to be on the expensive side, and a good fermenting crock can run upwards of $200 for one with a large capacity, but you generally get what you pay for. Good fermenting crocks are well-built, have lids that are sealed with a water gutter and come with a built-in weighting system that fits the crock perfectly. They also look great sitting on your counter. Just don't forget to replenish the water in the gutter during long ferments. The gutters don't hold a lot of water and air will be able to freely travel into the crock if the water used to create the seal is allowed to evaporate.

If you're on a budget or you're on the fence and aren't sure whether you want to ferment your own vegetables, Mason jars are your best choice. They're cost-effective and can be repurposed if you decide you don't want to ferment anymore. I'd at the very least invest in airlock lids for the jars because they're so much more convenient. Once you're comfortable fermenting and have decided it's something you want to do, you can invest in a nice crock or a few of the nicer airlock containers.

## Kraut Pounder (aka Cabbage Crusher)

If you've never made sauerkraut, you probably have no clue what a kraut pounder is. A *kraut pounder* is a wooden rod with a rounded knob at the end that's use to crush cabbage that's going to be turned into sauerkraut. They're usually made from a milled block of wood and the better pounders have different-sized knobs on each end to accommodate different sizes of containers.

Kraut pounders are nice to have if you plan on making a lot of sauerkraut because they speed up the task of crushing the cabbage. The cabbage is crushed in order to get it to release its natural liquid, so it can be used as brine. Kraut pounders are also used from time to time to bruise other vegetables in order to get them to release their inner juices.

These handy tools get the job done quickly, but they aren't an absolute necessity. Any blunt object can be used to mash cabbage. I used the blunt end of a small rolling pin for many years before someone gifted me a kraut pounder. I have a friend who uses one of the small wooden baseball bats they hand out at baseball games from time to time. If you don't have a kraut pounder, I'm sure you can come up with something you can use to crush cabbage. When all else fails, pick it up and squeeze it. That works, too.

## Weighting Systems

*Weighting systems* are weights designed to hold the vegetables you're fermenting beneath the surface of the brine, ensuring they don't come in contact with open air. Fermenting crocks and some of the other more expensive fermenting systems come with weights that are designed to fit snugly into the vessel, but for the most part you're on your own when it comes to figuring out how to hold the vegetables under the brine.

There are commercially-produced weights available for most jar and container sizes, but they tend to be expensive. You can spend as much as $30 to $40 for just a few weights. They're well-built, have smooth edges and they get the job done, but with a little ingenuity you can come up with a weighting system that costs a fraction of that.

You're going to need a smooth object made from a non-reactive material that's safe to come in contact with your food. It needs to be heavy enough to stay in place when you press it into the fermenting vessel. I've seen dinner plates and saucers used to good effect in larger fermenting vessels. The plate or saucer is placed in the vessel and something heavy is placed on top of it to hold it down. In smaller vessels, I've seen bags of rocks, bags of marbles, glass discs and even flat, smooth river stones all used to good effect.

Avoid using items made of wood, rough stone or other porous materials because they're difficult to clean and can harbor bacteria that can cause problems. Metal is also out of the question because it can react to the acids in the brine and plastic should be avoided because it can leach chemicals into the brine and contaminate it.

Regardless of the weighting system you decide to use, it needs to do one simple thing: keep the vegetables beneath the surface of the brine. Make sure it fits snugly into the vessel you're using it in, so a few rogue pieces of vegetable aren't able to escape and float to the top. You're going to want to make sure it's heavy enough to stay submerged when gas bubbles float up and attach to it. A convex surface will work better than a concave one in this regard. Bubbles will roll to the sides of a convex surface instead of building up beneath them, like they do with a concave surface.

## Cutting Instruments

When it comes to cutting instruments, the only instrument you absolutely have to own is a good, sharp knife. A good knife will make short work of most vegetable cutting and paring tasks and can be the only cutting tool you use, if need be. That said, there are a handful of other instruments that will make your life a lot easier if you have them on hand.

The second instrument I would purchase is a *food mandolin*. Mandolins are used to slice vegetables in a uniform thickness. There are attachments available that will allow you to julienne vegetables or to crinkle cut them. They're usually adjustable, so you can choose the thickness at which you want to slice the vegetable. If you're planning on doing thin slices, a mandolin may save your fingers!

Another cutting tool that'll save you a lot of work in the long run is a food processor. You'll be able to quickly shred or chop vegetables into small pieces instead of having to cut them by hand. A blender will work in a pinch, but a food processor is more versatile and you'll have more options at your disposal.

# How to Tell When Fermenting Is Complete

Ah, the age-old fermenting question. "*When is it done?*"

Every new fermenter asks this question and pretty much every new fermenter is unsatisfied with the answer they receive in response. The answer to this question is it's done when you think it's done.

Remember when I said fermentation is more an art form than it is a science? This is where that statement really comes into play. As vegetables ferment, more and more probiotic cultures develop. Longer ferments result in more robust probiotic profiles and larger amounts of beneficial bacteria in the food. While you may be tempted to ferment vegetables for as long as you possibly can in order to maximize the amount of probiotics you get with each serving, there are a couple good reasons you might not want to.

For one, vegetables that are left to ferment for longer periods of time will have significantly more lactic acid in them than those left to ferment for a shorter period of time. The longer you leave vegetables to ferment, the sourer they get. This may be a desirable trait for some people, while others will prefer their vegetables to have only a slight tang to them. You'll be getting a decent dose of probiotics either way, so it really boils down to personal preference.

Another consideration that must be made is the softness of the vegetables. Most people want their fermented vegetables to remain at least somewhat crisp. When left to ferment at room temperature for too long, vegetables will go soft. I've had to throw out a few batches of vegetables that I forgot about and didn't discover until they were extremely soft. Would they have been safe to eat? More than likely yes, but I couldn't bring myself to chew them up and swallow them.

Fermentation recipes give time ranges instead of exact time frames for good reason. The taste of vegetables after a few days at room temperature is all some people can handle, while others prefer the way their fermented vegetables taste after a lengthy fermentation. Additionally, factors like heat, brine strength and whether or not a starter culture was used can all affect how fast vegetables ferment.

There's no standard time at which they're done. They're ready when you say they're ready.

Another question that comes up often is how one can tell whether fermentation has taken place at all. Once you've successfully fermented a vegetable, you'll know exactly how to tell whether it's done or not in future batches. Until then, here are the three main signs that indicate a vegetable is fermenting:

- **Bubbling.** Bubbles are usually the first visible sign of lactofermentation. As the lactobacteria act on the carbohydrates in the vegetables, they create gases that rise to the surface of the container. There may only be a few bubbles rising to the surface or the brine could look like a carbonated soda. Either way, it's an indication that fermentation is occurring. I usually wait until the bubbling has slowed to a crawl to move my vegetables to cold storage.

- **Smell.** When you open a properly-fermented batch of vegetables, you'll be presented with a bouquet of aroma that's much different than what the vegetables smell like under normal conditions. Fermented vegetables take on a distinct sour smell that may be a little off-putting at first. Don't mistake this for the putrid stench of rotting vegetables. If your vegetables smell rotten, throw them out.
- **Taste.** Fermented vegetables take on a tangy, almost-effervescent flavor that's tough to mistake for anything else. The longer they're left to ferment, the more acidic they get.

The key to determining when your vegetables are done is to find the point in the fermentation process where you like them the best. Once you've been doing this for a while, you'll be able to trust your instincts and will know when your ferments are done. For now, err on the side of caution. If you put a batch of vegetables into the fridge early, they'll continue to slowly ferment and will end up just fine. Put one in too late, on the other hand, and there's nothing you can do to save it.

## Don't Forget to Burp Your Airtight Jars

Fermenting creates a lot of gas. This gas, in turn, creates pressure inside the jar.

When you're using airlock containers, this gas is released before it can build up a lot of pressure and isn't a problem. When you're using containers that are completely airtight, the gas can really start to build up, creating a significant amount of pressure.

I've heard wily fermenting veterans talk about containers that have popped their lids off with so much force they left a dent in the ceiling. I've also heard of jars literally shattering under the pressure, probably as a result of a chip or small crack in the jar that went unnoticed.

I've never seen either of these phenomena occur myself, but I have suffered one ill consequence due to built-up pressure. I used to have white curtains in my kitchen. The key phrase in that sentence is *used to*, because one day I was fermenting a batch of beet kvass and I forgot about it for a couple of days. I moved the jar from the cabinet to the counter to check my ferment and proceeded to open it. Beet kvass sprayed everywhere. If you've ever shaken up a can of soda and popped the top, the off-gassing of the kvass was similar to that, only on a much larger scale. It sprayed all over me and all over the kitchen. If you've never seen beet kvass before, it's a deep red, almost purple color—and it doesn't easily come out of fabric.

Learn from my mistakes and always off-gas your fermenting vegetables. I recommend opening the jar at least once every couple of days. There may still be some pent-up pressure in the jar, so place a towel over it when you open it. That way, any brine that sprays out will be trapped beneath the towel.

Once you move fermented vegetables to cold storage, the fermentation process slows enough to where you really don't have to worry too much about gases building up. Until then, be careful and be sure to open your airtight containers every once in a while. Your curtains will be all the better for it.

# Fermenting Recipes

The rest of the book contains fermenting recipes you can try out on your own. As far as ingredients go, don't be afraid to experiment. If there's something about a recipe you don't care for, feel free to change it. You can add and remove spices, mix different types of vegetables and create your own concoctions to your heart's content.

Don't limit yourself to just the recipes in the book. They're a good start, but I've discovered some of my best recipes when I've decided to forgo the conventional recipes and try something new. If you try something new and don't care for it, there's always next time.

These recipes assume you have a large enough fermenting vessel to make everything in a single batch. If not, you can divide the recipe up between multiple vessels. It helps if you mix everything first, so you don't have to guess how much to put in every jar.

## Easy Sauerkraut

We'll start off with the easiest recipe in the book. This recipe only requires 2 ingredients and is a great way to get your feet wet in the world of fermenting. If you're new to the game, this is as good a place as any to get started.

For an interesting look, try using one purple cabbage and one green one. It doesn't make a difference with the flavor, but looks great if you plan on serving the kraut to someone you're looking to impress. You can also use all purple or all red cabbage to create an aesthetically-pleasant kraut. Again, there's no real change to the flavor.

### Gather the following ingredients:

2 heads of cabbage
2 tablespoons Himalayan sea salt

### Here are the instructions for making easy sauerkraut:

1. Chop or shred the cabbage.
2. Add the cabbage to a bowl and use a kraut pounder or another blunt object to bruise the cabbage. Add the sea salt to the bowl and mix it into the cabbage.
3. Cover the cabbage and let it sit for 3 to 4 hours. It will release its natural juices and should create enough brine to where you don't need to add any water.
4. Transfer the contents of the bowl to the fermenting vessel. Weight the vessel and make

sure the cabbage is pressed beneath the brine. If not, put the lid on the container and store it in a cool, dark place overnight. By morning, there should be plenty of brine in the cabbage. If you still don't have enough brine, create 2% brine and add it to the fermenting vessel until the weight is covered.

5. Press the weight down to make sure there are no air pockets left in the cabbage. Leave 1" headspace at the top of the container.
6. Seal the fermenting vessel.

Store the vessel in a cool, dark place for 1 to 2 weeks. After a week has passed, check the kraut once a day and transfer it to cold storage once it's fermented to your preference.

## Fermented Coleslaw

Take the previous recipe and add coleslaw dressing and shredded carrots to it and you end up with cultured coleslaw. The carrots can be shredded and added before you ferment the sauerkraut or you can wait until the day you actually make the coleslaw.

I've used Greek yogurt instead of mayonnaise to make the recipe healthier than it would be if mayo was used. If you'd like, you can substitute half of the Greek yogurt for mayo to end up with more traditional coleslaw. I've tried it both ways and it's good either way.

**Gather these ingredients:**

4 cups fermented sauerkraut
2 cups Greek yogurt
4 tablespoons apple cider vinegar
2 tablespoons raw honey
1 teaspoon fresh dill, chopped
1 teaspoon Mrs. Dash original seasoning
Sea salt and black pepper, to taste

**Follow the directions to make fermented coleslaw:**

1. Combine all of the ingredients except for the sauerkraut in a bowl and stir them together.
2. Add the sauerkraut to the bowl and mix until it's coated with the dressing.
3. Chill and serve.

## Sweet & Sauerkraut

Combine apples with a traditional sauerkraut recipe and what do you end up with? A sweet and sour kraut recipe that is undeniably good. As long as you don't ferment them until the sugar in the apples has been completely consumed, you'll end up with sauerkraut that has a slight sweetness to it every time you bite into one of the apple chunks.

### Gather the following ingredients:

2 heads of organic cabbage
5 organic apples
2 teaspoons fresh ginger, grated
1 teaspoon cloves
OPTIONAL: Starter culture

### 3% brine (if necessary):
1 ½ tablespoons Himalayan sea salt
4 cups water

### Follow these directions to prepare the sauerkraut:

1. Wash the outside of the cabbage. Shred or chop the cabbage into thin strips.
2. Add the cabbage to a bowl and bruise it with a kraut hammer. Add the sea salt to the bowl and mix it in.
3. Cover the bowl and let it sit for a couple hours, giving the salt time to work its magic and pull moisture from the cabbage.

4. Wash the apples and grate them with the skin still on them. Add the apples, ginger and cloves to the bowl with the cabbage. Stir everything together.
5. Place the contents of the bowl into the fermenting vessel.
6. Add starter culture at this time, if you want to use it. Cabbage typically has enough cultures on the leaves to ferment on its own, but cultures can be added if you'd like.
7. Press the cabbage into the vessel to remove any air pockets. Place a weight into the fermenting vessel and press it down until the weight is submerged beneath the surface of the brine. If the cabbage didn't create enough brine of its own when the salt was added, make 3% brine and add enough of it to the container to cover the weight.
8. Leave 1" of headspace at the top of the container. Seal the container so it's airtight.

Ferment the sauerkraut in a cool, dark place for 5 to 7 days. Move it to the fridge when it's ready.

# Traditional Kimchi

*Kimchi* is a Korean dish that, like sauerkraut, is made from cabbage. The taste of kimchi is very different from that of sauerkraut because the *kochukaru*, or red pepper powder, imparts a spicy flavor. When you choose a red pepper powder, make sure you check the label. If there's anything but red peppers in the ingredient list, skip it and buy a different brand.

### Gather the following ingredients:

1 large head of green cabbage, sliced
1 Daikon radish, peeled and shredded
5 green onions, chopped
5 cloves garlic, chopped
¼ cup kochukaru (red pepper powder)
1 tablespoon soy sauce
2 teaspoons fresh ginger, grated
2 ½ tablespoons Himalayan sea salt

### Here are the directions for making kimchi:

1. Slice the cabbage into strips and put it in a bowl. Add the sea salt to the bowl and stir it into the cabbage. Use a kraut pounder to bruise the cabbage. Cover it and let it sit overnight.
2. In the morning, dump the contents of the bowl into a fermenting vessel. Add the radish, green onions and garlic to the vessel.

3. Combine the kochukaru, soy sauce and ginger and mix them together. Add the sauce to the fermenting vessel and mix it into the vegetables.
4. Weight the kimchi down, so that all of the vegetables are beneath the surface of the brine. Leave 1" headspace.
5. Seal the vessel.

Ferment the kimchi at room temperature for 1 to 2 days before moving it to the fridge. Let it sit in the fridge for another week or two before eating it.

# Daikon Radish Kimchi

Daikon radish kimchi is a fresh-tasting kimchi that uses white Korean radishes instead of cabbage. It's great when served alongside grilled steaks or chicken and is a tasty addition to salads.

**Gather the following ingredients:**

2 pounds Daikon radishes
2 carrots, shredded
5 cloves garlic, peeled and chopped
4 green onions, chopped
Starter culture

**2% brine (if necessary):**
1 tablespoons Himalayan sea salt
4 cups water

**Here are the directions for making Daikon radish kimchi:**

1. Cut the tops and bottoms off of the radishes. Peel them and slice them into thin slices.
2. Add the radishes to the fermenting vessel, along with the carrots, garlic and onions.
3. Create the brine and pour it over the top of the vegetables. Add a couple tablespoons of whey, a starter culture packet or half a cup of juice from a previous ferment to the vessel.

4. Weight the vegetables down to ensure they stay beneath the surface of the brine. Leave 1" of headspace in the container.
5. Seal the vessel.

Place the fermenting vessel in a cool, dark place and let the kimchi ferment for up to a week. Check it once every couple of days and get rid of any foam that develops. Move the kimchi to cold storage when it's ready.

# Cortido

It seems like pretty much every country in the world has a traditional fermented cabbage dish that's been in existence for ages. *Cortido* is a Latin American fermented cabbage dish that somehow manages to taste completely different from both kimchi and sauerkraut.

Cortido adds *kohlrabi* to the mix. If you've never used kohlrabi before, this is a great way to acquaint yourself with it. It's a crisp, juicy vegetable and both the greens and the root are edible. Peel the skin and the tough, fibrous outer layer of the kohlrabi root away before using it in this recipe.

**You're going to need the following ingredients:**

1 cabbage, shredded
2 carrots, grated
1 kohlrabi, peeled and grated
1 tablespoon kohlrabi greens, chopped
3 green onions, chopped
2 teaspoons oregano
1 teaspoon red pepper flakes
2 tablespoons whey

**3% brine (if necessary):**
1 ½ tablespoons Himalayan sea salt
4 cups water

**Follow these instructions to make cortido:**

1. Place the cabbage into a bowl and pound it with a kraut pounder to get it to release its juices. Add the cabbage to the fermenting vessel.
2. Combine the rest of the ingredients and add them to the fermenting vessel.
3. Cover the cortido with brine and place a weight on top, so the vegetables are held underwater. Leave 1" headspace in the vessel.
4. Seal the vessel.

Ferment at room temperature for up to a week. Start checking the cortido after 4 days. When the cortido is fermented to your liking, transfer it to cold storage.

## Fermented Kale and Cabbage

We round out the cabbage recipes with a recipe that combines kale and cabbage. I literally eat this recipe right out of the jar, it's so good. It's also good when added to salads or served over rice, if you can save it until dinnertime.

**Gather the following ingredients:**

1 cabbage, chopped
3 cups kale, stemmed and chopped
1 onion, chopped
2 cloves garlic
1 teaspoon lemon juice

**5% brine:**
2 ½ tablespoons Himalayan sea salt
4 cups water

**Here are the directions for making fermented kale and cabbage:**

1. Prepare the vegetables. Remove any large stems from the kale and discard them. It's OK to leave the smaller stems intact.
2. Add the vegetables to the fermenting vessel.
3. Make 5% brine and pour it over the vegetables until they're covered.
4. Weight the vegetables down until they're completely submerged beneath the brine. Leave 1" of headspace.

5. Seal the vessel.

Ferment the kale and cabbage at room temperature for up to a week. Check the kale and cabbage daily after 4 days have passed and move it to cold storage once it's ready.

## Fermented Asparagus

Here's a quick and easy way to put up extra asparagus you harvested (or purchased from the store). The growing season for asparagus in the area where I live is short and asparagus is only available at good prices for a limited time. I grow a bunch of it and buy even more of it when it's on sale. One of the ways I preserve it is by fermenting it, so I'll have asparagus to eat well into winter.

**Gather the following ingredients:**

15 to 20 asparagus spears
3 cloves garlic, peeled and chopped
½ teaspoon mustard seeds
1 teaspoon dill seeds
½ teaspoon red pepper flakes

**4% brine:**
2 tablespoons Himalayan sea salt
4 cups water

**Here are the directions for making fermented asparagus:**

1. Cut the tough ends off of the asparagus. Cut the asparagus down to size, so they'll fit in the jar. You can either stand them up in the jar or chop them into 2" to 3" pieces and fill the jar with the pieces.
2. Add the rest of the ingredients to the jar.

3.  Create 4% brine and pour it over the asparagus. Make sure the brine covers the asparagus.
4.  Weight the asparagus down, so it's held under the brine by the weight.
5.  Seal the vessel.

Ferment the asparagus at room temperature for up to 2 weeks. Check the asparagus daily after a week. Move it to cold storage once it has fermented to your preference.

## Fermented Brussels Sprouts

When I first attempted to ferment Brussels sprouts, I wasn't sure whether the characteristic bitterness of the sprouts would get in the way of the tangy flavor associated with most fermented vegetables. Never in a million years did I think this recipe would turn out as good as it did.

Not only does the bitterness not get in the way; it's almost completely eliminated during fermentation. Fermented Brussels sprouts are good enough to snack on, or you can add them to soups and salads. Make sure you add them to the soup when you serve it. Cooking them will kill the good bacteria.

**Gather the following ingredients:**

2 pounds Brussels sprouts
4 green onions, thinly sliced
2 garlic cloves, peeled and chopped
½ teaspoon red pepper flakes

**5% brine:**
5 tablespoons Himalayan sea salt
8 cups water

**Here are the directions for fermenting Brussels sprouts:**

1.  Slice the Brussels sprouts in half. Add them to the fermenting vessel, along with the rest of the ingredients.

2. Create 5% brine and pour it over the top of the Brussels sprouts until they're completely covered.
3. Weight the sprouts down, so they're held beneath the surface of the brine.
4. Seal the vessel.

Ferment the sprouts for up to week. Check them daily after the 4th day and move them to cold storage when they've fermented to your preference.

## Fermented Garlic Radishes

I've never been a big fan of the biting bitterness of radishes. I used to eat them from time to time in salads and may have had them a handful of times when they were presented at a friend's house for dinner, but I've never gone out of my way to eat a radish.

I was caught off-guard by this recipe because I actually liked it. Fermenting radishes takes away some of the bite, smoothing the flavor out enough to where it doesn't punch you in the taste buds.

### Here are the ingredients you're going to need:

10 to 15 radishes, sliced
4 garlic cloves, peeled and chopped

### 4% brine:
2 tablespoons Himalayan sea salt
4 cups water

### Follow these directions to ferment radishes:

1. Add the radishes to the fermenting vessel, along with the garlic.
2. Create 4% brine and pour it over the radishes and garlic until they're covered.
3. Place a weight over the radishes and garlic and press it down until it's holding them under the surface of the brine.
4. Seal the vessel.

Ferment the radishes at room temperature for up to week. Check the radishes periodically and transfer the radishes to cold storage when they're ready. The longer they ferment, the less bite they'll have.

## Cultured Carrots

Since you're peeling the carrots for this recipe, you're going to want to add starter culture. This holds true for most vegetables, as the beneficial bacteria usually reside in larger amounts on the peel.

**You're going to need the following ingredients:**

10 carrots
Starter culture

**3% brine (if necessary):**
1 ½ tablespoons Himalayan sea salt
4 cups water

**Follow these instructions to make cultured carrots:**

1. Peel the carrots and cut them into sticks.
2. Add the carrots to the fermenting vessel.
3. Create the brine and pour it over the carrots.
4. Add the starter culture to the vessel. A couple tablespoons of whey or a packet of vegetable starter culture works well.
5. Add the weight to the vessel and make sure it's holding the carrots under the brine. There should be around 1" headspace.
6. Seal the vessel.

Ferment the carrots for up to 14 days in a cool, dark place. Start checking the carrots after 8 days and move them to cold storage when they're ready.

## Fermented Ginger Carrots

This recipe probably isn't one you're going to want to snack on by itself because of the large amount of ginger used, but it's a great addition to salads and to fermented coleslaw. Eat a little bit at a time, as a little bit of this recipe goes a long way.

### Here are the ingredients you're going to need:

8 to 10 carrots, peeled and shredded
3 tablespoons fresh ginger, grated
3 tablespoons whey

### 2% brine:
1 tablespoon Himalayan sea salt
4 cups water

### Follow these directions to ferment the ginger carrots:

1. Combine the carrots and the ginger. Add them to the fermenting vessel.
2. Create 2% brine and pour it over the carrots until they're covered. Stir it slowly to get rid of any air pockets in the shredded carrots.
3. Add the whey to the fermenting vessel.
4. Place the weight in the vessel and press it down until it's holding the carrots and ginger beneath the surface of the brine. Leave 1 ½" headspace.
5. Seal the vessel.

Ferment the ginger carrots at room temperature for 3 to 5 days. Transfer to the fridge when they've fermented to your preference.

## Dilly Carrots

Take the previous recipe and make a few minor changes and you end up with the traditional American dish known as dilly carrots. The garlic in this recipe is optional, but does add a bit more flavor to the carrots.

### Here are the ingredients you'll need to gather:

5 carrots, cut into sticks
4 garlic cloves, chopped
1 tablespoon fresh dill, chopped
Starter culture

### 3% brine:
1 ½ tablespoons Himalayan sea salt
4 cups water

### Follow these directions to make dilly carrots:

1. Peel the carrots and cut them into sticks.
2. Add the carrots to the fermenting vessel, along with the garlic cloves and the dill.
3. Create your brine and pour it over the carrots.
4. Add the starter culture to the vessel. A couple tablespoons of whey or a packet of vegetable starter culture work well.
5. Add the weight to the vessel and make sure it's submerged. Leave an inch of headspace.
6. Seal the vessel.

Ferment the carrots for up to a week in a cool, dark place. Start checking the carrots after 4 days and move them to cold storage when they're ready.

## Dilly Beans

Here's another traditional American dish, popular across large stretches of the Midwest. This recipe is similar to dilly carrots, but uses green beans instead. I've also tried this with string beans fresh from the garden and it worked well.

**Here are the ingredients you're going to need:**

2 pounds of fresh green beans
4 cloves garlic, chopped
2 tablespoons dill seeds

**5% brine:**
2 ½ tablespoons Himalayan sea salt
4 cups water

**Follow these directions to ferment dilly beans:**

1. Cut the ends off the green beans and break them in half. Place them into the fermenting vessel.
2. Add the garlic and the dill seeds to the vessel.
3. Create 5% brine and pour it over the beans until they're covered.
4. Weight the beans down, so they're submerged beneath the surface of the brine. Leave 1" of headspace.
5. Seal the vessel.

Ferment the dilly beans at room temperature for up to 5 days. Start checking them after 3 days and move them to cold storage once they've fermented to your preference.

## Dilly Sugar Snap Peas

Here's yet another dilly recipe. This one, however, isn't so traditional, as I've only seen it in a handful of places. This recipe is best consumed within a week or two of creating it, while the snap peas are still nice and crisp. If you wait too long, they'll start to go soft and will take on a strong sour taste.

**Here are the ingredients you're going to need:**

1 to 2 pounds snap peas
4 garlic cloves, peeled and chopped
1 tablespoon oregano
½ teaspoon dill seeds

**5% brine:**
2 ½ tablespoons Himalayan sea salt
4 cups water

**Follow these directions to ferment snap peas:**

1. Trim the ends off of the peas. Pack whole peas into the fermenting vessel.
2. Disperse the garlic cloves, oregano and dill seeds throughout the peas.
3. Create 5% brine and pour it over the peas until they're covered.
4. Weight the peas down, so they're beneath the surface of the brine. Leave 1" of headspace.
5. Seal the vessel.

Ferment at room temperature for 2 to 4 days. Check the peas once a day after the 2$^{nd}$ day and move them to cold storage once they've fermented to your preference.

## Fermented Onions

If you regularly consume raw onions, then I can't think of a good reason why you shouldn't replace regular raw onions with fermented onions. They taste great and have worked well in every recipe I've tried them in.

These onions can be used in cooked recipes, but cooking the onions will kill the probiotic bacteria. I recommend using them in salads, on sandwiches and as part of other dishes that call for raw onions.

Feel free to switch the flavor up by adding garlic or your other favorite herbs and spices.

**Gather the following ingredients:**

4 large red onions, sliced into rings

**5% brine:**
2 ½ tablespoons Himalayan sea salt
4 cups water

**Here are the directions for making fermented onions:**

1. Slice the onions into thin rings. Thinner rings will ferment better than thicker rings.
2. Add the onions to the fermenting vessel.
3. Create 5% brine and pour it over the onions.
4. Weight the onions down until they're submerged beneath the surface of the brine.
5. Seal the fermenting vessel.

Ferment the onions at room temperature for up to a week. Check them daily after 4 days and move them to cold storage once they've fermented to your preference.

## Lactofermented Yellow Summer Squash

When I first tried to ferment summer squash, I had no clue what to expect. I half-expected them to turn into mushy slime within a week. Instead, they stayed firm and crisp and were delicious, but don't take my word for it. You've got to try this recipe yourself to believe it.

### Here are the ingredients you're going to need:

4 yellow summer squash
5 cloves garlic, peeled and chopped
1 tablespoon fresh basil, chopped
Starter culture

### 4% brine:
2 tablespoons Himalayan sea salt
4 cups water

### Follow these directions to ferment summer squash:

1. Slice the squash into coins. Alternatively, cut the squash into sticks.
2. Place the squash and the garlic into the fermenting vessel.
3. Chop the basil and add it to the vessel.
4. Create 4% brine and pour it over the squash until they're covered.
5. If you're using starter culture, now's the time to add it. Use 2 tablespoons of whey, a vegetable culture packet or half a cup of liquid from a previous ferment.

6. Weight the squash down. Be sure to leave 1" of headspace.
7. Seal the vessel.

Ferment the squash for up to 4 days at room temperature. Once the squash are ready, move them to cold storage.

## Zucchini Pickles

Once I tried fermenting summer squash and was able to do it successfully, I knew zucchini was going to be a success as well. Here's a recipe you can use to make zucchini pickles, which are a nice deviation from the cucumber pickles you're accustomed to.

**Here are the ingredients you're going to need:**

4 zucchini
3 cloves garlic, peeled and chopped
2 tablespoons fresh dill, chopped
2 tablespoons pickling spices
Starter culture

**4% brine:**
2 tablespoons Himalayan sea salt
4 cups water

**Follow these directions to ferment summer squash:**

1. Slice the zucchini into strips. Smaller zucchini can be quartered.
2. Place the zucchini, garlic, dill and pickling spices into the fermenting vessel.
3. Create 4% brine and pour it over the zucchini until they're covered.
4. If you're using starter culture, now's the time to add it. Use 2 tablespoons of whey, a vegetable culture packet or half a cup of liquid from a previous ferment.

5. Weight the zucchini down. Be sure to leave 1" of headspace.
6. Seal the vessel.

Ferment the squash for 3 to 5 days at room temperature. Check the zucchini pickles daily after the 3$^{rd}$ day and move them to cold storage when they're ready.

## Sweet Pickles

*Sweet pickles*, also known as *bread and butter pickles*, are tart and tangy at the same time. If you've never tried lactofermented pickles, you're in for a special treat. They're much better than the pickles you buy from the store that have been pickled in vinegar.

If you want dill pickles instead of sweet pickles, eliminate the sugar and add an extra teaspoon of dill.

**Here are the ingredients you're going to need:**

8 to 10 pickling cucumbers
½ teaspoon mustard seeds
1 teaspoon dried dill
A few peppercorns
3 tablespoons whey
2 tablespoons cane sugar or rapadura

**3% brine:**
1 ½ tablespoons Himalayan sea salt
4 cups water

**Follow these directions to prepare the pickles:**

1. Slice the cucumbers into coins or strips.
2. Add the cucumbers to the fermenting vessel. Leave enough space for the weight.
3. Add the rest of the ingredients to the vessel.
4. Pour brine over the cucumbers until they're submerged.

5. Place the weight into the vessel and press it down until it's beneath the surface of the brine. Leave an inch of headspace at the top of the vessel.
6. Seal the vessel.

Ferment the pickles in a cool, dark place for up to a week. Check them daily after 3 days and transfer them to cold storage once they've fermented to your preference.

## Fermented Vegetable Medley

I decided to see what would happen if I picked a selection of my favorite vegetables, threw them into a fermenting vessel and let them ferment for a few days. I was surprised by how good the resulting ferment actually tasted. Try this vegetable medley as it stands or see if you can come up with a better one on your own.

### Gather the following ingredients:

2 cups cauliflower florets
2 cups broccoli florets
1 carrot, sliced
1 onion, chopped
4 cloves garlic, minced
1 tablespoon ginger, grated

**5% brine:**
2 ½ tablespoons Himalayan sea salt
4 cups water

### Here are the directions for making the fermented vegetable medley:

1. Break the cauliflower florets and broccoli florets into smaller pieces.
2. Combine the vegetables and mix them together. Add them to the fermenting vessel, along with the garlic and ginger.
3. Make 5% brine and fill the vessel until the brine is covering the vegetables.

4. Weight the vegetables down. Press the weight down until the vegetables are completely submerged. Leave 1" of headspace.
5. Seal the vessel.

Ferment the vegetable medley at room temperature for 3 to 5 days. Start checking the vegetables after 3 days. Move the fermented vegetables to cold storage once they've fermented to your preference.

## Layered Veggies

While most fermented vegetables look cool when they're fermented in a glass container, this recipe ups the cool factor by layering the vegetables to create an aesthetically-pleasing arrangement. Ferment these vegetables in a nice jar and place a great-looking label on them and you've got a gift you can give to almost anyone.

### Gather the following ingredients:

1 cup radishes, sliced into coins
1 cup carrots, sliced diagonally
1 cucumber, sliced into coins
1 cup green beans
Enough red or purple shredded cabbage to fill the rest of the container

**5% brine:**
2 ½ tablespoons Himalayan sea salt
4 cups water

### Here are the directions for fermenting layered veggies:

1. Prepare the vegetables. Arrange them in layers in the fermenting vessel. Top the veggies off with enough fermented cabbage to almost fill the container. Make sure you leave room for the weight.
2. Create 5% brine. Pour enough brine into the container to cover the vegetables.

3. Weight the vegetables down until they're below the surface of the brine.
4. Seal the vessel.

Ferment the vegetables for 3 to 5 days. Start checking them daily after 3 days and move them to cold storage when they're fermented to your preference.

## Pickled Mexican-Style Vegetables

If you've ever been to a Mexican restaurant that serves pickled vegetables, this recipe is probably pretty close to what you were served. This recipe doesn't just taste great; it's remarkably bright-colored and looks amazing.

### Gather the following ingredients:

7 large radishes, sliced into coins
1 pickling cucumber, sliced into coins and then halved
2 jalapenos, sliced into coins
4 carrots, peeled and shredded
½ cup cilantro, chopped

### 5% brine:
2 ½ tablespoons Himalayan sea salt
4 cups water

### Here are the directions for fermenting Mexican-style vegetables:

1. Prepare the vegetables and arrange them in the fermenting vessel. Disperse the cilantro amongst the vegetables.
2. Make the brine and add it to the vessel until the vegetables are covered.
3. Place a weight in the container and press it down until it's holding the vegetables beneath the surface of the brine.
4. Seal the vessel.

Ferment the vegetables for 3 to 5 days. Check them daily after 3 days and move them to cold storage once they have fermented to your liking.

## Pickled Peppers

Pickling peppers dulls the heat of the pepper and makes eating spicy peppers a less arduous ordeal. I'm a big wuss when it comes to spicy food and even I can enjoy the light warmth and mingled flavors of a good pickled pepper.

There are a handful of ways peppers can be pickled. This recipe covers three of the most popular ways. The peppers you choose to pickle are entirely up to you, as these methods will work with most edible peppers. If you want the final product to be less spicy, remove the seeds from the peppers before fermenting them.

Peppers are best when fermented in 5% brine. Add 2 ½ tablespoons of sea salt to 4 quarts of water to make brine for your pepper recipes.

**Here are the directions for pickling whole peppers:**

1. Place the whole peppers into the fermenting vessel, stems and all.
2. Cover the peppers with 5% brine.
3. Weight the peppers down. Add more brine if necessary to cover the weight. Make sure you maintain at least an inch of headspace.
4. Seal the vessel.

Ferment whole peppers for 7 to 10 days before moving them to the fridge. Age them for 4 to 6 months before consuming them.

**Here are the directions for pickling pepper slices:**

1. Trim away the stems and the tips of the peppers.
2. Slice the peppers into coins.
3. Place the peppers into the fermenting vessel.
4. Cover the peppers with 5% brine.
5. Weight the peppers down. Leave 1" of headspace.
6. Seal the vessel.

Ferment the peppers for 7 to 10 days before moving them to the fridge. Transfer them to the fridge and allow them to age for an additional 4 to 6 months.

**Last, but not least, here are the directions for fermenting pepper paste:**

1. Trim the stems and tips away from the peppers.
2. Place the peppers into a blender or food processor and blend until smooth. Keep your face away from the blender or food processor, as the fumes can be pretty intense.
3. Weigh the peppers to see how much they weigh.
4. Multiply the weight by 0.10 and add that weight of Himalayan sea salt to the peppers. Blend it in.
5. Transfer the pepper paste to the fermenting vessel. Leave 1" of headspace.
6. Seal the vessel.

Ferment the pepper paste for 5 to 7 days before moving it to the fridge. Stir the pepper paste once a day to prevent mold from forming. Let the paste age for 4 to 6 months in the fridge.

## Habanero Hot Sauce

First, a warning. This stuff is hot. Extremely hot. Habanero peppers won't just burn your mouth when you eat them, the oils from the peppers can get on your skin when you're working with them and can then be transferred to your eyes or any other sensitive area you decide to touch and can burn the skin.

Wear gloves when working with these peppers and don't forget to take them off before rubbing your eyes or going to the bathroom.

If you're into hot sauce, this is a great sauce. If you don't like spicy food, stay far, far away from this cultured hot sauce. The culturing process may dull the heat from the peppers a bit, but habanero peppers are hot no matter what you do to them.

### You're going to need the following ingredients:

5 habanero peppers
10 large jalapeno peppers

**4% brine (if necessary):**
1 tablespoon Himalayan sea salt
2 cups water

**Follow these instructions to make habanero hot sauce:**

1. Cut the stems and the ends off the jalapeno peppers. Remove the stems from the habanero peppers.

2. Place the peppers into a food processer or blender and blend until smooth.
3. Dump the pepper puree into the fermenting vessel.
4. Make 4% brine and add enough of it to cover the pepper puree.
5. Place the weight into the container and use it to hold the puree beneath the surface of the brine.
6. Seal the vessel.

Ferment at room temperature for 5 to 7 days. Move to cold storage and let the sauce sit for another week before you eat it. Give it a good stir before using it.

## Cultured Green Tomatoes

If you grow tomatoes in a cold climate, you know the frustration of watching fall rapidly approach while you still have green tomatoes on the vine. Instead of culling the plants and throwing out those green tomatoes, they can be fermented into a tasty probiotic snack.

**Gather the following ingredients:**

5 cups of green cherry tomatoes
1 onion, chopped
3 bay leaves
4 cloves garlic, minced
2 teaspoons dill seeds
½ teaspoon celery seed
½ teaspoon mustard seeds
¼ teaspoon allspice
½ teaspoon coriander seeds
¼ teaspoon ground cinnamon
2 whole cloves

**5% brine:**
5 tablespoons Himalayan sea salt
8 cups water

**Here are the directions for making cultured green tomatoes:**

1. Poke a couple holes in each of the tomatoes using a sewing needle or a toothpick.

2. Fill the fermenting vessel with the tomatoes. Add the rest of the ingredients to the vessel.
3. Make 5% brine and pour it over the top of the cherry tomatoes.
4. Add the weight to the container and press it down until it's beneath the surface of the brine. Add more brine if you need to. Leave about 1" of headspace.
5. Seal the vessel.

Ferment for up to a week in a cool, dark place. Start checking after 4 days and move the tomatoes to cold storage once they're ready. These tomatoes really come into their own when they're left alone in the fridge for an additional 2 to 3 weeks.

## Cultured Grape Tomatoes

I planted way more tomato plants than I needed this year. About three-quarters of the way through the growing season my friends and family were so sick of tomatoes I couldn't give them away. I didn't want to throw them out, so I decided to preserve them.

This is one of the recipes I used. It's a quick and painless (unless you miss with the needle) way to preserve large amounts of tomatoes.

### Gather the following ingredients:

4 cups of grape tomatoes
2 tablespoons fresh basil, chopped

**5% brine:**
2 ½ tablespoons Himalayan sea salt
4 cups water

### Here are the directions for making cultured green tomatoes:

1. Poke a hole in each of the tomatoes using a clean sewing needle or a toothpick.
2. Fill the fermenting vessel with the tomatoes. Add the basil to the fermenting vessel.
3. Make 5% brine and pour it over the top of the grape tomatoes.
4. Add the weight to the container and press it down until it's beneath the surface of the brine.

Add more brine if you need to. Leave about 1" of
headspace.
5. Seal the vessel.

Ferment for 5 to 7 days and then transfer to cold storage.

## Lacto-Salsa

I've got a serious weakness for a good salsa and this salsa is so good it's irresistible. If you like your salsa on the spicy side, add another jalapeno or two. If you're feeling particularly sadistic, add a habanero pepper. Make sure you wear gloves when handling the peppers.

**Gather the following ingredients:**

3 tomatoes, diced
1 onion, diced
1 bell pepper, diced
2 jalapeno peppers, diced
2 cloves of garlic, chopped
2 tablespoons lime juice
2 teaspoons Himalayan sea salt

**Here are the directions for making lactofermented salsa:**

1. Combine all of the ingredients in a bowl and mix them together.
2. Dump the contents of the bowl into a fermenting vessel.
3. Place the weight in the vessel. If there isn't enough water to submerge the weight, add water until the weight is covered. Leave 1" of headspace.
4. Seal the container.

Ferment the salsa for up to 4 days in a cool, dark place. Once you're happy with where the salsa is at, move it to cold storage.

## Fermented Salsa Verde

This recipe switches things up a bit by swapping out the tomatoes in the previous recipe for tomatillos, which are green tomatoes. This green salsa is every bit as easy to make as the previous recipe and it's every bit as good. The only problem I have now is deciding which of the two salsas I want to make.

**Gather the following ingredients:**

2 pounds tomatillos
1 onion, chopped
1 jalapeno pepper
2 cloves of garlic, minced
½ cup cilantro
1 tablespoon fresh lime juice
1 tablespoon Himalayan sea salt

**Here are the directions for fermenting salsa verde:**

1. Remove the husk from the tomatillos and dice them.
2. Combine all of the ingredients in a bowl and mix them together.
3. Dump the contents of the bowl into a fermenting vessel.
4. Place the weight into the vessel. If there isn't enough water to submerge the weight, add water until the weight is covered. Leave 1" of headspace.
5. Seal the container.

Let this salsa ferment for up to 10 days. Check it periodically after 7 days have passed and move it to cold storage once it's ready.

## Lacto-Ketchup

I've always been a huge fan of ketchup, but I had to stop eating it a few years back because I would get terrible heartburn and stomachaches every time I ate it. Once I learned what was in commercial ketchup, I understood why. It may have been made from tomatoes at one point, but the stuff you're squeezing out of the bottle isn't anything close to the healthy vegetable it once was.

I was a little skeptical when I was told lactofermented ketchup would probably be fine for me to eat, even though I couldn't tolerate the commercial stuff. It turned out to be fine and I've been able to add ketchup back to my diet. I no longer have to check labels and worry about what's in my ketchup. I know I'm getting the real deal and it's made from all-natural ingredients.

### You're going to need the following ingredients:

1 sixteen-ounce can tomato sauce
2 six-ounce cans of tomato paste
1 fresh tomato, boiled and crushed
2 teaspoons garlic powder
2 teaspoons onion powder
3 tablespoons maple syrup
A pinch of cayenne pepper
½ teaspoon black pepper
1 tablespoon Himalayan sea salt
4 tablespoons whey

### Follow these directions to make lacto-ketchup:

1. Combine all of the ingredients in a blender and blend them together. Make sure they're completely blended.
2. Place the ketchup into the fermenting vessel. Seal the vessel. There's no need to use a weight on lactofermented ketchup.

Allow the ketchup to ferment for 2 to 3 days. Give it a good stir before you transfer it to cold storage.

## Lacto-BBQ Sauce

Take the previous recipe and add a handful of ingredients to it and you end up with lactofermented BBQ sauce that's a pretty good replacement for the high fructose corn syrup-laden sauces sold in stores.

**Here are the ingredients you're going to need:**

1 sixteen-ounce can tomato sauce
2 six-ounce cans of tomato paste
1 fresh tomato, boiled and crushed
2 teaspoons garlic powder
2 teaspoons onion powder
1 tablespoon dried mustard
2 tablespoons apple cider vinegar
3 tablespoons maple syrup
2 tablespoons raw honey
A pinch of cayenne pepper
1 tablespoon lemon juice
½ teaspoon chili powder
½ teaspoon black pepper
1 tablespoon Himalayan sea salt
4 tablespoons whey

**It looks like a lot of ingredients, but the directions are fairly simple:**

1. Combine all of the ingredients in a blender and blend them together. Make sure they're completely blended.

2. Place the BBQ sauce into the fermenting vessel. Seal the vessel. There's no need to use a weight on lactofermented BBQ sauce.

Allow the sauce to ferment for 2 to 3 days. Give it a good stir before you transfer it to cold storage.

## Cultured Horseradish

Horseradish isn't for the weak of heart. It's strong enough to make your eyes tear up and there's no mistaking the distinct flavor of this potent root when it's added to pretty much any dish you can think of.

I wish I could tell you fermenting horseradish dulls it a bit and makes it more tolerable. It doesn't…But if you're already a fan of horseradish, this is a great way to add probiotics to your diet.

**Gather the following ingredients:**

2 cups fresh horseradish root, peeled and chopped
Starter culture
2 tablespoons Himalayan sea salt
Water, as needed

**Here are the directions for making cultured horseradish:**

1.  Peel and chop the horseradish root into chunks.
2.  Add the horseradish root, starter culture and sea salt to a blender or food processor and pulse until combined.
3.  Add water a tablespoon at a time and pulse until the horseradish root forms into a thick paste. Keep adding water and blending it in until the horseradish is the consistency you want it to be.
4.  Place the horseradish into the fermenting vessel. Add water to the vessel to fill it to within an inch of the top of the jar.

5. Seal the vessel.

Ferment the horseradish at room temperature for up to a week. Start checking it after 4 days and move it to cold storage when it's fermented to your preference. This is going to be a tough one to determine when it's ready because most people aren't going to want to sample it on its own to test it.

## Fermented Walnut Pesto

Use this pesto in dishes where you don't cook the pesto or you run the risk of killing off the probiotic bacteria with the heat used to cook it. It works well as a dip for raw vegetables and can be served over most salads to good effect. I've also added it to sliced deli meat sandwiches and love the flavor it adds to them.

### Gather the following ingredients:

3 cups fresh basil leaves
3 cloves garlic, peeled and chopped
½ cup extra-virgin olive oil
½ cup walnuts

### 4% brine:
1 tablespoons Himalayan sea salt
2 cups water

### Here are the directions for making fermented walnut pesto:

1. Place the basil leaves and garlic into the fermenting vessel.
2. Create 4% brine and pour it over the basil leaves.
3. Weight the leaves down, so they're held under the brine by the weight. Leave 1 ½" of headspace at the top.
4. Seal the vessel.

Ferment the pesto for a week at room temperature. Once it's done fermenting, add it to a blender with the olive oil and the walnuts. Pulse until it's the consistency you want it. Store the pesto in an airtight container in the fridge.

## Fermented Garlic Cloves

Fresh garlic has a pungent smell and can have a biting, bitter taste. Some people love it and some people hate it. I fall strongly into the former, while my husband falls into the latter category. There's just something about garlic he doesn't care for.

Fermenting garlic takes away much of the bite, leaving it mellow and smooth. My husband still isn't in love with it, but he'll eat it when I use it to make garlic toast.

**Gather the following ingredients:**

Garlic heads (as many as you want to ferment)
3 tablespoons whey

**3% brine:**
1 ½ tablespoons Himalayan sea salt
4 cups water

**Follow the directions to ferment garlic cloves:**

1. Gently break open each of the garlic heads. Separate all of the cloves.
2. Bring a pot of water to a boil. Place the garlic cloves into the pot of water and boil them for 30 seconds. Transfer the cloves to an ice water bath to stop them from continuing to cook.
3. Remove the paper covering each of the cloves. Place the cloves into the fermenting vessel.

4. Prepare the 3% brine. Pour the brine over the cloves. Make sure all of the cloves are covered with brine.
5. Add the whey to the fermenting vessel.
6. Weight the cloves down. Leave 1" of headspace at the top of the vessel.
7. Seal the vessel.

Ferment garlic cloves in a cool, dark area for up to a week. Transfer them to the fridge and allow them to age for another 3 to 4 months.

## Miso-Fermented Garlic

*Miso paste* is a Japanese dish made by fermenting soybeans. It's a staple in Japanese cuisine that is used to impart the flavor of umami to the dishes it's added to. This recipe calls for red miso, but works just as well with white miso. Try them both and see which you like better. The mirin in this recipe is optional. *Mirin* is a sweet rice wine that's a staple in many Japanese dishes.

I like to crush this recipe and mix it with melted butter to create cultured miso-garlic butter.

**You're going to need the following ingredients:**

1 pound garlic cloves
2 cups red miso paste
3 tablespoons whey
OPTIONAL: 3 tablespoons mirin

**Follow these directions to ferment this recipe:**

1. Peel the garlic cloves. Boil them for 30 seconds and transfer them to an ice water bath to stop them from continuing to cook.
2. Add the miso and mirin to a bowl and stir it together. Add the whey and stir it in.
3. Place a layer of miso in the bottom of the fermenting vessel. Place a layer of garlic cloves on top of the miso. Cover the garlic with another layer of miso. Press the layer of miso into the garlic to ensure there are no air pockets.

Continue alternating layers of miso and garlic until you reach the top of the container. The last layer should be a layer of miso. Leave 1" of headspace at the top.
4. Seal the container.

Ferment the miso-garlic for up to a week. Store the garlic-miso in the fridge for at least 6 months before you eat it.

## Fermented Garlic Scapes

In addition to the bulb, the scapes of the garlic plant can be harvested and fermented. The *scape* is the green flower stalk that grows out of the ground when the garlic is preparing to bloom.

Scapes for salads are best when harvested while they're young and tender. Scapes harvested for fermenting purposes are no different. Harvest them while they're small or you'll end up with a woody stalk that's barely edible.

**Gather the following ingredients:**

Garlic scapes (as many as you want to ferment)

**2% Brine:**
1 tablespoon Himalayan sea salt
4 cups water

**Follow these directions to ferment garlic scapes:**

1. Cut away any woody sections of the scapes and discard them. Cut the scapes into 2" to 3" pieces. Wash the scapes and place them into the fermenting vessel.
2. Make 2% brine and pour it over the scapes.
3. Weight the scapes down. Make sure you leave 1" of headspace in the container.
4. Seal the container.

Ferment the scapes at room temperature for 3 to 5 days. Start checking them after 3 days and move them to cold storage once they're ready.

## Beet Kvass

No vegetable fermentation book would be complete without a recipe for beet kvass, a traditional Ukrainian beverage that is typically consumed with meals.

Traditional beet kvass is usually made with only beets. This recipe adds cabbage and onion in order to add an additional dimension to the flavor of traditional kvass. If you want to try traditional kvass, leave out the carrots and the onion. Be forewarned…it tastes strongly of beets. If you like beets, that's great. If beets aren't at the top of your list of favorite vegetables, add the onion and cabbage to dull the strong beet flavor a bit.

**Gather these ingredients in order to make beet kvass:**

3 beets, peeled and chopped coarsely
Half a cabbage, chopped
Half an onion, chopped
OPTIONAL: Starter culture

**4% brine:**
2 tablespoon Himalayan sea salt
4 cups water

**Follow these directions to make beet kvass:**

1. Add the vegetables to a fermenting vessel.
2. Create 4% brine and pour it over the top of the vegetables.

3. Add the starter culture and stir it in if you plan on using it. A few tablespoons of whey or a starter culture packet work well for this recipe. If you've already got beet kvass on-hand, you can use half a cup of kvass as starter culture as well.
4. Weight the vegetables down so they stay under the brine. Leave 1" of headspace.
5. Seal the vessel, so it's airtight.

Ferment the beet kvass at room temperature for up to a week. Taste it daily after 4 days have passed and move it to the fridge when it's ready. When you want to drink it, strain out the vegetables and drink the liquid.

# Frequently Asked Questions

This section seeks to answer some of the most common questions asked by fermenters. There are a handful of common occurrences you should be aware of, so you aren't caught off-guard.

### What Should I Do With the Brine?

Brine can be consumed, but it does contain a significant amount of salt and may not be a good choice for those on a salt-restricted diet. It can also be combined with olive oil and vinegar to make salad dressing. The best use for brine is to use it as a starter culture for future ferments. Once you start getting low on fermented vegetables, use a cup or more of brine from the vegetables you have on hand to get the next batch started.

### Why Aren't My Vegetables Fermenting?

There are a number of reasons why you might be having trouble getting vegetables to ferment. Here are some of the more common reasons:

- **Antibacterial products were allowed to come in contact with the fermenting vessel.** If this happens, wash the vessel out really well and try again.

- **You're trying to ferment in too hot of an area.**
  Lactobacteria start to die when temperatures
  climb above 80° F. Get too much over this
  temperature and you may kill the bacteria before
  they have a chance to start growing.
- **You're trying to ferment in too cold of an
  area.** Fermentation will slow to a crawl as
  temperatures drop below 60° F. The colder it
  gets, the slower the bacteria move. If you're
  fermenting in too cool of a location, fermentation
  may still be taking place, albeit at too slow of a
  speed for it to be noticeable. Move the
  vegetables to a warmer area and fermentation
  should speed up.
- **There are problems with the bacteria in the
  vessel.** Sometimes you can do everything right
  and something still goes wrong. If you just can't
  seem to get a ferment to kick off, dump the
  vegetables and try again. If you didn't use a
  starter culture, try using one the next time
  around.

*Why Is There Foam Forming at the Top of the
Container?*

When ferments are particularly vigorous, it isn't
uncommon for foam to form at the top of the container.
Scoop it out and discard it. The foam should dissipate as
the vegetables near the end of the initial ferment.

### Why Aren't There Many Bubbles in the Container?

Some ferments bubble more than others. It's just the nature of the beast. As long as you're able to see some bubbles and the food is taking on the characteristic sour smell of fermented food, then fermentation is taking place.

### Why Is There White Stuff Floating at the Top of the Container?

The white sediment you're seeing is probably yeast. It can be scooped out and discarded with no harm done to the fermenting vegetables. Don't leave it in the container, as it can cause some vegetables to take on a yeasty flavor.

### Is It OK to Ferment on the Counter?

That depends on the container you're fermenting in. If the container is made of a clear material, you're going to want to ferment in the dark. On the other hand, if you're using a container into which light is unable to penetrate, fermentation can be done on the counter, as long as it doesn't get too cold or hot in the area where you're fermenting.

### Does the "Lacto" In Lactofermentation Mean Dairy Products Are Involved?

No, the term "lacto" refers the lactobacteria that are responsible for fermentation. The only time dairy products are added is if you add them yourself. Be aware dairy is sometimes used as a carrier in vegetable starter culture packets.

### Can I Use Vinegar in My Ferments?

Not if you want truly lactofermented vegetables. Vinegar disrupts the fermentation process and changes the environment in the vessel. You'll end up with pickled foods instead of fermented foods. If you want to use vinegar, add it when you serve the fermented vegetables.

### What Causes Vegetable Ferments to Spoil?

Here are some of the risk factors that may cause your fermented vegetables to spoil:

- **Not enough salt in the brine.**
- **Stems and blossom ends weren't removed.**
- **The container or utensils weren't sterilized.**
- **The person preparing the food didn't wash his or her hands.**
- **The vegetables were left at room temperature in a warm room for too long.**
- **The vegetables weren't properly weighted and floated above the brine.**
- **The wrong type of salt was used.**
- **The wrong type of water was used.**

- There were already brown spots on the vegetables.
- Using too ripe of vegetables.
- Yeast was allowed to grow unchecked in the brine.

# Works Cited

1. **Wanjek, Christopher.** Doctors Detect Obesity Bug on Breath. *LiveScience.* [Online] 3 26, 2013. [Cited: 4 1, 2014.] http://www.livescience.com/28176-obesity-bug-detected-on-breath.html.

2. **Kresser, Chris.** 9 Steps to Perfect Health - #5: Heal Your Gut. *Chris Kesser: Health for the 21st Century.* [Online] [Cited: 4 1, 2014.] http://chriskresser.com/9-steps-to-perfect-health-5-heal-your-gut.

3. *Diversity of the human gastrointestinal tract microbiota revisited.* **Rajilic-Stojanovic, M, Smidt, H and de Vos, WM.** 9, s.l. : Environ Microbiol, Sep 2007, Vol. 9.

4. **Mercola, Dr.** This Food Contains 100 TIMES More Probiotics than a Supplement . *Mercola.com.* [Online] 5 12, 2012. [Cited: 3 23, 2014.] http://articles.mercola.com/sites/articles/archive/2012/05/12/dr-campbell-mcbride-on-gaps.aspx.

5. **Ramaley, Dr. David.** Benefits of Fermentation. *Seattle Natural Health.* [Online] [Cited: 2 21, 2014.] http://www.seattlenaturalhealth.com/fermentation.html.

6. *Prevention of neural tube defects: results of the Medical Research Council Vitamin Study.* **Unknown.** 8760, s.l. : Lancet, 1991, Vol. 338.

7. **Unknown.** choline. *The World's Healthiest Foods.* [Online] The George Mateljan Foundation. [Cited: 4 12, 2014.] 2014.

8. **Hyman, Dr. Mark.** Glutathione: The Mother of All Antioxidants . *Huffington Post.* [Online] 4 10, 2010. [Cited: 2 21, 2014.] http://www.huffingtonpost.com/dr-mark-hyman/glutathione-the-mother-of_b_530494.html.

9. **Unkonwn.** Jarisch-Herxheimer reaction. *Wikipedia.* [Online] [Cited: 2 5, 2014.] http://en.wikipedia.org/wiki/Herxheimer_reaction.

10. *Probiotics and their fermented food products are beneficial.* **Parvez, S, et al., et al.** s.l. : Journal of Applied Microbiology, 2005. ISSN 1364-5072.

11. *Probiotics for treating acute infectious diarrhoea.* **Allen, Stephen J, et al., et al.** s.l. : Cochrane Database Syst Rev, 2010. doi: 10.1002/14651858.CD003048.pub3.

12. *Meta analysis of lactic acid bacteria as probiotics for the primary prevention of infantile eczema.* **Zhu, DL, Yang, WX and Yang, HM.** 9, s.l. : Zhongguo Dang Dai Er Ke Za Zhi, Sep 10, 2010, Vol. 12, pp. 734-9.

13. *Efficacy of Lactobacillus Rhamnosus GR-1 and of Lactobacillus Reuteri RC-14 in the treatment and prevention of vaginoses and bacterial vaginitis relapses.* **Cianci, A, et al., et al.** 5, s.l. : Minerva Ginecol, 2008, Vol. 60, pp. 369-76.

14. *Effect of a dietary supplement containing probiotic bacteria plus vitamins and minerals on common cold infections and cellular immune parameters.* **Winkler, P, et al., et al.** 7, s.l. : Int J Clin Pharmacol Ther., Jul 2005, Vol. 43, pp. 318-26.

15. *Clinical effects of Lactobacillus acidophilus strain L-92 on perennial allergic rhinitis: a double-blind, placebo-controlled study.* **Ishida, Y, et al., et al.** 2, s.l. : K Dairy Science, Feb 2005, Vol. 88, pp. 527-33. PMID: 15653517.

16. *Oral delivery of Lactobacillus casei Shirota modifies allergen-induced immune responses in allergic rhinitis.*

**Ivory, K, et al., et al.** 8, s.l. : Clin Exp Allergy, 2008, Vol. 38. PMID: 18510694.

17. **Unknown.** Natural Fermentation: Salt vs. Whey vs. Starter Cultures. *Cultures for Health.* [Online] [Cited: 2 11, 2014.] http://www.culturesforhealth.com/compare-salt-whey-starter-culture-ferment-vegetables-fruits-condiments.

18. **Michaelis, Kristen.** Are Mason Jar Ferments Safe? . *Food Renegade.* [Online] [Cited: 4 15, 2014.] http://www.foodrenegade.com/mason-jar-ferments-safe/.

Printed in Great Britain
by Amazon